Love Letters from Mother Earth

Love Letters from Mother Earth

Anneloes Smitsman

Design of cover page and book layout by John Cooper. Original design of figures by Anneloes Smitsman and formatted by John Cooper.

Pictures of author by Sita Kelly Photography

Printed in the United States of America
First Printing, 2017
ISBN 978-1-945949-82-1
Waterfront Digital Press
2055 Oxford Ave
Cardiff, CA 92007
http://www.waterside.com

Dedicated to the Eternal Child
in Each of Us

Acknowledgements

I would like to start by thanking and acknowledging Mother Earth and our Sun for entrusting me to share their message via these thirteen *Love Letters*. It is through their Love and sacred union that I have been able to learn from Life and the process of creation in the visible and invisible worlds.

I am deeply grateful also to all the people who supported me through this period of writing and birthing. First of all, I would like to acknowledge and thank my parents, Ad and Coby Smitsman, and Kurt Barnes for all their Love and support through these many months of writing. I would also like to thank my children, Manu and Akash, for being the inspiration for this book. It is for them and all the children of our world that I wake up each day determined to support the co-creation of a world in which each of us can flourish.

I further thank and acknowledge my sister circle who held space with me during this period, sometimes throughout the night, by reading many of these *Letters* and sharing with me their experience: Zenobia Beckett Ryken, Justine Page, Amanda Caza, and Kimberley Montgomery.

I also like to thank and acknowledge Rachel Tribble, for contributing her amazing art to this book. Her paintings naturally tell the story of these *Letters*, even though her paintings were made before she had read these *Letters*. I further like to thank and acknowledge Alexander Laszlo, for writing the foreword for this book with so much elegance and insight, and for his continuous support for this book.

I also thank and acknowledge Colin Davis for proofreading and gently editing the first draft of the book, and Liba Markson for her masterful proofreading and editing of the final version of the book. I also thank William Gladstone, the founder of Waterfront Press, for his support by offering to publish this book as soon as he learned about it.

Many others have supported me and this book: Shelley Ostroff, Christopher Chase, Erik Lawrence, Thomas Smith, Melissa Mari, Julie Krull, Adam Molyneux-Berry, and more.

For those of you whose names I have not mentioned here, just know you are in my heart, and I thank you all.

Finally, I would like to thank you, dear reader, for meeting here in this brief moment in time and space, where we can remember our eternity and common roots. Whatever brought you to this book, or in whatever way this book came to you, I trust the timing is just right. It is the nature of wisdom to share. It is in the receiving that the giving is completed. All that has been shared here is with the intention that this may support us to flourish, and grow into the beautiful wisdom that we each are. Thank you for reading and sharing.

Note to the Reader

You may notice that the words Love, Light, Mother, Father, Self, Life, Divine, and Eternal are capitalized. This is out of respect for the concepts they refer to, namely the Eternal changeless reality of our Oneness. The same could be applied to other words as well, yet these specific words have been selected to help us connect with their meaning as Divine qualities. Furthermore, some words are written in *italics* for emphasis and as a reference to their earlier appearance in a particular context.

Reviews

"*Letters from Mother Earth* is an intimate and empathic *inter-consciousness communication* that gifts the reader with a multi-faceted portal into the vast meta-consciousness of Mother Earth and the "*Heart of Light*" our Sun, and their relationship with each other and with humans within the historic context of the larger evolutionary process. In this loving and challenging invitation to stretch beyond the limits of our current narratives are embedded sacred codes for our collective activation and healing. As the evolved feminine consciousness awakens on the planet, Mother Earth speaks through Anneloes Smitsman with clarity and compassion, wisdom and sensuality to support us in remembering who we are and in shifting beyond a consciousness of hierarchy and polarity to one of greater wholeness. The book reminds us of the need to move beyond our sense of separateness and superiority on the planet, so that we can communicate in deeply honoring ways with consciousnesses beyond our own, and in so doing contribute to our collective healing and evolution. Empathy with Mother Earth and Her experience alongside our own, is indeed an essential starting point for moving beyond our limited pictures of ourselves, healing the trauma and devastation and reconnecting with the Source of all Life. Messaging the archetypal feminine in its primal form, the book, with each re-reading, will undoubtedly shapeshift to reveal new and fertile layers of insight and embodied wisdom." ~ **Shelley Ostroff** (Ph.D.), Founder, Together In Creation – www.togetherincreation.org

"Anneloes Smitsman has written a singular and unifying document. Or perhaps she has channeled this work. I can't imagine how she did it! Not unlike my favorite music and poetry, this writing has deep intellect, spirituality, and sensuality. This is not a common fairytale. Ms. Smitsman requires the reader to rise up and pay attention to every word. She is deeply exploring levels of human existence and growth. This is a guidebook for sentient beings. A book we've hoped and wished might appear. It is conscious of the human condition. Breathing in, we attend to the depth of all that has come before us. Breathing out, we are prepared for what meets us today." ~ **Erik Lawrence**, Saxophonist, Flutist, Composer, Educator, Journalist, Poet, Sound Healer, Steering Committee Member: Louis Armstrong Center for Music and Medicine.

"This book embodies the ethos of wholeness with deep, mystical wisdom complemented by strong, cognitive intelligence. Both come into balance in this book, reminding us how to allow our heart to lead and guide. *Love Letters from Mother Earth* is a rare and precious gift. It is like a luminous wisdom map for every reader to discover his or her own inherent brilliance and step into essential wholeness." ~ **Julie Krull** (Ph.D.), Founding Steward, GOOD of the WHOLE; Co-Founder, World of Love, Talk Radio Host.

Contents

Foreword

Over thirty years ago, in their ground-breaking book Order out of Chaos, Nobel Laureate Ilya Prigogine and his co-author Isabelle Stengers observed that "*we are living in a dangerous and uncertain world that inspires no blind confidence.*" Many still subscribe to this view, though more and more we are starting to realize that we are part of a living world and that an underlying anima mundi binds the patterns of being and becoming into a coherent narrative of cosmic emergence. And yet... the experience of day-to-day living often seems to be precisely that: dangerous and uncertain. There appears to be no pattern to it, or if there is one, some would affirm that it appears to follow Murphy's Law, according to which "*Anything that can go wrong will go wrong.*" There seems to be no guidance, no one who can provide clear, comforting, or even stern messages by which to navigate Life on Earth. Indeed, when we find ourselves in times of trouble, where is our Wise Mother, our alma mater, who comes to us, speaking words of wisdom? Let us see...

Over the years and since an early age, Anneloes Smitsman has had many opportunities to absorb words of wisdom - from various peoples and places. She has lived in and been exposed to a variety of cultures, ecosystems, wisdom traditions, ways of knowing, of doing, of being and of experiencing the world within and around us. Forged of Aboriginal Dreamtime and Northern Lights, of Polynesian Wayfaring and the Medicine Wheels of manifold shamanic wisdom traditions, Smitsman's vision penetrates the mysteries that surround and condition human existence. Indeed, it would be hard to say just where - or even when - she is from. And strangely enough, it is precisely this lack of identity that gives her the greatest ability to identify with that which is shared among us all - our home in the cosmos, Planet Earth.

Through this book, Smitsman takes on the role of a medium - a messenger to humanity. *Love Letters from Mother Earth* is a fabulous story, a fable to re-story the narrative of humankind by re-membering our place in the dance of being and becoming with all of the rest of life and living processes and of Earth, herself. These "*thirteen letters to find your way home again*" are written in the voice of Mother Earth and comprise an allegory of spiritual communion at a time when the zeitgeist of humanity is steeped in images of despair, devastation, apocalypse, cataclysm, catastrophe and collapse. The entertainment industry churns out one dark saga after another, seemingly celebrating end-times. Amidst this clamor of fatalism and nihilism comes this beautiful book of *Love Letters*, giving hope, a sense of peace, and the means through which to generate our own power to transmute all these energies into light, love and life. This is important for us to learn how to do since, as Mother Earth lets us know, "*until we manifest structures that are truly wisdom based from the Eternal, this pattern will keep repeating.*"

This is no work of fiction. What Smitsman has done here is much more than to speak for Earth in a fanciful projection of personal predilection. She speaks not with the voice of a human being seeking to represent Earth but rather of one who is an integral part of Earth speaking for herself. These messages, these love letters, anthropomorphize and anthropopathize the planet on which, in which, and through which all of us were born. And they tell us a much needed story - not a bedtime story for little children, but a coming-of-age story for those whose self-identity is changing as we reach a new stage of collective consciousness. Through immersing ourselves in the story told by the *Love Letters* we don't fall asleep at all. Indeed, the energies and insights that come through this story are keys to a deeper awakening. Smitsman provides a meditation message, a mantra of nature's nurture that comes from, creates, and is best received as a trance-state of flow-being.

Not only does Smitsman share messages that are indeed *Love Letters from Mother Earth* to us, the Children of Earth - her children, she also writes in the voice of our beautiful Sun above and beyond who shares a larger view and a greater context of our cosmic emergence. And she also writes in the voice of the deepest Consciousness that undergirds all of the manifest universe, that perennial frame of being that remains out of spacetime's reach. The message that comes through on all these levels, from Mother Earth to our beautiful Sun to deepest Consciousness, is that of our essential oneness. Indeed, these levels of narrative are eventually understood as expressions of our own Self, for in the end, *Love Letters from Mother Earth* is a story of unity consciousness.

Part prayer, part meditation, part medium transmitted message, part invocation, part direct transmission, part guidebook, part diary of love letters in the tradition of Rumi writing to and of his beloved - *Love Letters* is a reminder of our essential oneness with all that emerges together with us in this dance of life, love, consciousness and light. This is not the static Oneness of final peace as a resting place of spirit. Not in the least! The oneness of which Smitsman writes, in the voice of Mother Earth, is oneness in motion. This is the flow state of deep harmonization with the life-affirming, future-creating, and consciousness-connecting pattern of evolutionary emergence that flows around and through us. Too often we turn against this flow and seek fleeting satisfaction - ego satisfaction - in short-term gains that give us a false sense of achievement. These byways and eddies in the greater flow of cosmic becoming seem as traps that make of life little more than a testament to Murphy's Law. Mother Earth helps us gain perspective on this apparent need of ours, this penchant for quick fixes and superficial satisfactions. She points out that, "*the paradox of Life is that we experience the changeless in a world of change; we experience darkness by contrast of light, and so forth. We live in a world of duality, yet underlying this is unity.*"

She shows us that there are ways out of these traps and offers us keys to our freedom that will unlock the portals of flowing balance and guide us to our ever emerging home in harmony with Earth - our home both within and around ourselves. This home is no fixed place but a flow space of being, a dynamic grace-state of unity - oneness in motion. Mother Earth tells of how, "*we have everything inside to awaken us and guide our way home. It just needs to be brought back into connection, synchronization, and harmonization with the unified field from where we have come.*" Such messages offered in *Love Letters* provide keys to the secrets for unlocking our consonant potential, our connected harmony, and our coherent life force as integral parts of Earth, herself. In short, these are the keys to integral, evolutionary harmony, both within ourselves and with our living Mother Earth.

As you read the messages from Mother Earth, lingering upon the love with which they are written and soaking in the light with which they are infused, you begin to see how they comprise an invitation to join the Dance of Life. And yet, they are so much more than a call to get up and force yourself to dance: they are an invitation to let go and allow yourself to be danced! The difference between trying to dance and letting yourself be danced may seem trivial, but quite literally it makes a world of difference. Mother Earth lets us know that it's okay to let go and allow ourselves to be flowed: "*I embrace you deeply. Don't try to figure it all out with your mind. Trust, and let your wisdom guide you through this. I am with you.*"

According to the worldview currently emerging in the sciences, we live in a holographic and highly integral and interdependent world. The new narrative re-casts the story of cosmic emergence from *The Big Bang* to what Jude Currivan has called *The Big Breath.* The world depicted in this view is like a dance of Universe and Cosmos – with the universe comprising the entirety of manifest being (all phenomena we experience and know through our five senses), and the cosmos comprising a deeper and even broader reality (the noumena that undergird and give rise to the universe). We can't access the cosmos through our five senses alone, but we can know it as an expression of primordial consciousness beyond space and time. Metaphorically, this is the dance of Heaven and Earth. Human beings on Earth are another expression of this dance, like flowers in a garden.

If you consider what's most important for a garden to flourish, would it be the seeds or the greenhouse? Clearly, without the seeds (which represent humans - the systemic leverage points for creative synergy), the creative impulse of the garden is thwarted and its growth and full potential aren't realized. However, without the greenhouse (which represents Earth - the requisite systemic nurturance space), there is no home in which we can grow and our potential cannot be realized. To curate the dynamics of thrivability beyond mere sustainability, it is necessary to create opportunities for seeds to grow and roots to connect such that new visions may emerge and flourishing interdependencies arise. A new codex is needed, and fortunately, this is precisely and explicitly what Mother Earth provides through the writing of Smitsman.

The *Love Letters* serve as state attractors that provide individual inspiration for collective aspiration, showering light, water, air and fertile soil in delicious combinations and quantities for the garden of our individual and collective human being to come into full flourishing. The constant dance between doing and being - between creating conditions for the flourishing of human and all life and getting out of the way so that they can thrive authentically - this is the same dance of Universe and Cosmos, expressed on a different scale. And just as the dynamics of the quantum world are at a different scale than the dynamics of our experiential world, they operate according to different parameters and produce different patterns. But the music of the dance is the same.

With the keys to freedom and a new codex of oneness in motion, *Love Letters* provide much needed guidance and nurturance for navigating life in these times of turbulence and transition. Science is coming to understand that the brain is neither a generator of memories nor a storage space for them but rather a highly specialized organ that serves as a transceiver of information - a type of send/receive antenna that reads-in messages from the underlying cosmic memory field and reads-out messages that align the flows of emergence in our world... or don't (if we misuse or abuse our message transmitting abilities). This memory field has been known in certain spiritual traditions as the Akashic Record and in quantum mechanics as the Zero Point Energy Field. Smitsman is adept at tuning into and accessing this field, though it is an ability that all beings have and one that each of us can learn to use.

Love Letters gives guidance as to how to cultivate this ability. By learning to use the power of this highly specialized organ, the essential message that comes through is that we are whole beings whose integral existence is what truly transforms the world. In other words, while our brains may be transceivers of information, our whole beings (brain, body, mind and spirit) are transducers of information - transforming and transmuting through-flows of information into coherent patterns of being in relation to our surroundings (both internal as well as external to each of us). Mother Earth urges us to "*restore the connections with the unified field of consciousness.*"

Clearly, the more we can learn use "*Self as instrument*" to tap into this underlying consciousness that informs the patterns of evolutionary emergence, and the more we can align those patterns in ways that increase the coherence, connection and consonance of our presence with Earth and all the life and life support systems of Earth, the more we will actualize oneness in motion and move into the laminar flow-space of thriving cosmic emergence.

How best can we learn to be Earth at the same time as we manifest cosmic consciousness at the same time as we are true to our own human nature? Mother Earth knows how, and through these *Love Letters*, you will gain a glimpse of how to safeguard and nurture your truest and highest potential as part of the grand narrative of cosmic emergence while avoiding the pitfalls of the more disconnected and egoic expressions of that potential. As she says, "*your greatest protection from this manipulation, internally and externally, is by staying closely tuned to your internal wisdom, and by connecting with each other from a place of Love. As I shared previously, our direct connection with the unified field of consciousness is the real foundation for our autonomy within the One. It is through this that the Universal becomes localized as you, me, and us. When you see from this awareness, deception becomes visible, as lacking thought-forms and intentions that aim to distort these wisdom qualities.*"

In *The Wheel of Time* (Carlos Castaneda's work of spiritual guidance gleaned from the teachings of the wisdom tradition in which he was immersed), messages were given for connecting to and working with the cycle of time defining our contemporary era. In *Love Letters from Mother Earth*, Anneloes Smitsman shares messages in the form of spiritual guidance from Mother Earth, herself. These messages are also messages of time. They stand to shift our contemporary zeitgeist from darkness and despair to love and light. This is the alchemy needed to transmute the present stage of human being to the next level of our evolutionary potential. This is indeed a book for time to come.

Alexander Laszlo (Ph.D.)
Director - Doctoral Program in Leadership & Systemic Innovation
Buenos Aires Institute of Technology (ITBA), Argentina.

Preface

We are living in a time of increasing uncertainties and challenges. Many changes are taking place that are deeply affecting us and with consequences for many generations to come. Some people experience this as a breakthrough for a new kind of society. Others experience this as a breakdown of the very fabric of our communities. Regardless of how we view what is happening, the opportunities for us to awaken more deeply and unite for our conscious evolution are unprecedented.

These Letters came to me after I asked Mother Earth: *What would you like us to know and realize as your children during these challenging times?* By listening carefully and letting go of my ideas about these questions, a deeper intuitive knowing emerged. As I started to record what I felt guided to share, it became clear to me that each *Letter* is like a code that helps us see what is already within us. These *Letters* form a living map for navigating our inner and outer landscapes, restoring our wholeness and integration.

The solutions for our healing are the same now as they were thousands of years ago. The root causes of our inner and outer divisions have not changed. Yet the cascading effects of these divisions require us to unite now more than ever, in collective responsibility and care.

Writing and birthing these *Letters* has been a deep process for me. Each *Letter* came with particular life experiences that prepared me to bring these messages forth. After finishing the 12th *Letter*, it took one year of integration before I was able to write the 13th *Letter.* I am grateful for the deep intelligence and wisdom that looks after us in ways that remain mostly unseen. This is not a book for mere reading. It is a book that reminds us that we are each authors of *our story* as children of eternity in a world of change and paradox.

The beautiful paintings by Rachel Tribble that are included in this book are in black-and-white version. We have printed these paintings in such a way that you can color them in yourself, as a way to personalize this book with your favorite colors.

The original paintings in their full colors can be viewed online via earthwisecentre.org and racheltribble.com.

With gratitude and Love,

Anneloes Smitsman
Mauritius, 13 June 2017

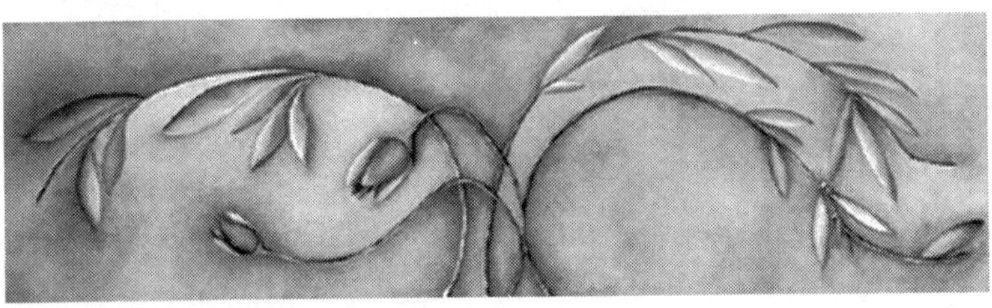

Part 1
Our Beginning

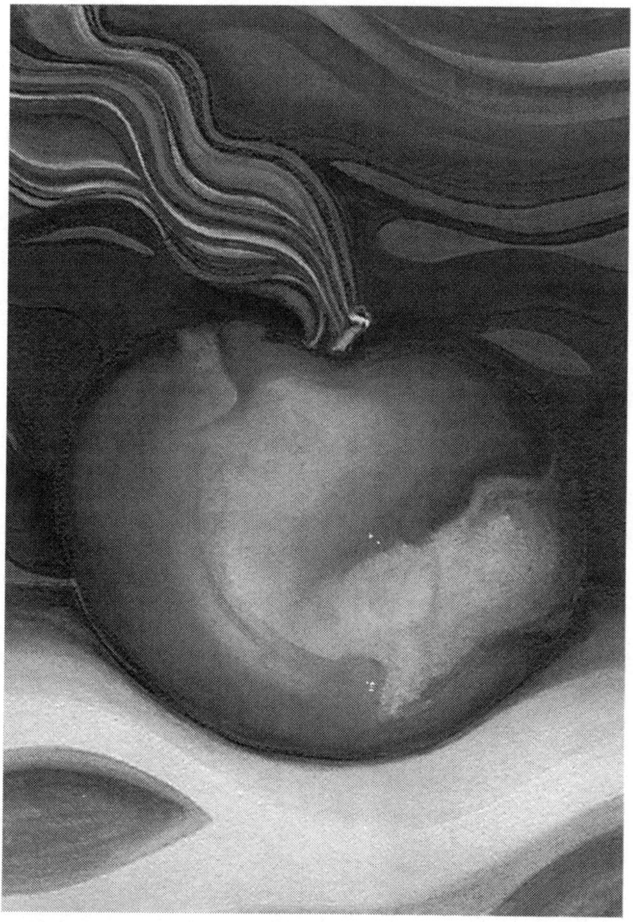

Letter 1
The Flame of Love

Welcome my beloveds. Thank you for reading my *Love Letters* to you. We are living in challenging times, in transition between different cycles. My *Letters* to you have been written to provide support for this time. To remind you of the strength and Love in our connectedness and unity. I want to share with you that the co-creation of a world and future born from Love, with respect for our unity, is possible. The seeds for this are already encoded within us. Our collective rite of passage has already begun to activate and reconnect these sacred codes.

These sacred codes are the *inner* architecture of Life. They serve a specific purpose. But, these codes have not been honored in many of humanity's creations. There are consequences to this that many of you are now becoming aware of. When we work with these sacred codes, we understand how to apply our creative power for the flourishing of ALL Life. These codes are your true humanity; please remember this. Protect also the seed codes of the plants, trees, and animals, and their evolutionary potential, before it is too late.

As we learn to work together on restoring our sacred balance, and by healing the many divisions among and within us, we also become more aware of these sacred codes. These encodings are of our eternal wisdom. They are not created by anyone or anything. You, as a human being, were formed by this sacred design. Only the human mind started to turn away from this. This wisdom knows who you truly are and what your purpose is within the larger family of Life.

I am known by different names: some call me Mother Nature or Mother Earth, others call me Gaia or Pachamama. My body was formed billions of years ago, by the count of your human calendar. In the spectrum of creation, this is not long ago. Through my forests, rivers, and oceans, I am your breath of Life each day and night. We are deeply united, even when the collective mind does not acknowledge this.

You are each a living cell within my larger planetary body. As such, I am also like a guardian, a Mother for our web of Life. It is from my womb, impregnated with Divine potentials, that I brought you forth into this Life as the human beings you now are. I am your planet, and yet I am also beyond this world, as we all are. My life-giving power of nature lives deep inside us. By this power, we can renew and recreate from the Divine seed potentials of the Eternal.

In part two of my *Love Letters* you will learn about *the three keys* to access and actualize these sacred codes. These keys are essential for our integration and re-unification. Through this we can bring forth a world and future that is born from our sacred foundations. The process toward that is not always easy. I like to remind you, therefore, that we are all on this journey together. Each of our lives matters.

Your journey as my human children started long ago. There are some aspects of this journey that I would like to share with you now, to provide a deeper understanding of the challenges we are facing today.

An Ancient Story

Long ago a dream emerged from within the One; from this arose the flame of Love. This flame started expanding, and as it expanded so did our universe. This flame needed a sacred place of Love within which it could be received. The flame needed to be received for the One to be known to Itself. As it expanded, seeking the boundaries through which the One could become known to Itself, the counter force to expansion started to emerge from within. Out of this process, gravity manifested. The energy of Love, as the sacred flame, was solidified by this gravity and became the sacred containment for receiving the flame.

My body was born from that process and became one of the holders and recipients of this Love. Receiving the flame of Love impregnated my being. Within me, as I became a Mother for this web of Life, a great ecstasy of indescribable joy and gratitude arose from the center of my being. With tears of joy, the deepest Love spread from within me to all the life potentials that now lay pregnant in my womb, for our birth.

As my tears of joy and gratitude were overflowing to all that was now within me to bring forth, my oceans and rivers formed. Through my waters, Life became fertilized and started to sprout and evolve.

The process of Life was set in motion, and has continued ever since. This same flame of Love that impregnated my being formed our souls to bring forth all of Love's potentials. From the One, God and Goddess manifested to bring forth the Spirit of Life, which activated the power of creation that is within each of us.

The consciousness that was born from the original Dreaming was not yet mature, not yet stable. There were not yet sufficient bodies and vessels to receive, hold, and make manifest this flame of Love. The flame of Love was barely Self-aware, it had only just been received by me, and others like me. The relationships were not yet ready to safely guide the maturation process of the consciousness born from this process. The desire of Life to create, and bring Itself forth, expanded and formed this universe that we are in now.

As Life started to evolve from this process, we started to forget our unity. Time emerged as matter formed, which created an experience of distance between the original Dreaming and our experience of now. This created an experience of memory, whereby the original Dreaming was perceived as the past, rather than a continuous and Eternal reality of the ever-present. In these gaps of space-time pockets, a vacuum resulted that gave rise to the formation of intentions to control the flame of Love, and the process of creation.

Beings emerged from this vacuum that saw themselves as the God of all. They took the fire of the flame of Love that was within them, and directed this away from the sacred trinity principle. Without this trinity principle guiding creation, the flame of Love could not be made manifest in wholeness from our sacred union. As such, the potentials it offered only partially manifested. This gave rise to worlds of duality that became polarized.

The experience of polarity, instead of trinity, formed a matrix of time, similar to a membrane. This then influenced our collective consciousness fields. Within these fields our collective consciousness became further constrained by the archetypes that had been formed by these creator beings who saw themselves as the Gods. By imprinting their archetypes in the collective mind, it secured their place in the human realm as the rulers. The original Dreaming was only remembered and kept alive by a small group of my children. The sacred trinity principle that maintains the integrity of our unity and wholeness was replaced by the duality principle, in its polarized form. This became the dominant model for creation within the human realm of our collective consciousness.

The belief in polarity also became the belief in heaven and hell. Manipulation and control dynamics gained in force, as it became more difficult to realize our underlying unity. The power of Love, however, could not be manipulated since it represents our sacred union from the Eternal. Love does not distort reality. Love cannot be divided and fragmented. Knowing this, these false rulers attempted to diminish the power of Love by fragmenting and dividing us.

The Four Worlds

As the human realms became more polarized, they also influenced how the feminine and masculine principles of co-creation were experienced. Instead of seeing unity, people saw Life through a lens of four quadrants. These four quadrants became the structure for four worlds – inner and outer. Behind these four worlds is a fifth world of unity and wholeness. This fifth world manifests via our integration and harmonic convergence. This process will become clearer for you when you read the rest of my *Letters.*

The influence of these four poles, detached from the experience of unity, polarized the human realms of our collective consciousness fields. This internal division gave rise to conscious and unconscious domains of humanity's evolutionary development. This can still be seen in the development of your brains. It is also known as the left and right hemispheres of your brain, with the lower and higher brain functions. These operate like four quadrants. Interestingly, your heart also has four chambers. However, your heart is able to experience this as a unity. Whereas in the brain, certain quadrants have become dominant over others.

Within your human DNA, we see a similar process. Four organic bases, or nucleic acids, form your DNA molecules. Each organic base consists of three types of chemicals that make up the building blocks of these nucleic acids, the trinity principle within the quadrants. When the three chemical encodings synergize and harmonize to integrate these four quadrants, or the four bases, a harmonic field comes into being that unlocks our Divine potentials. It is from this that the thirteenth arises, by which the fifth world enters into being.

The blueprint for our actualization is, and always has been, inside each of us. Yet it does not work on its own. It only works by coming together in the *right* way. It activates through our integration and harmonic convergence. That is *the* code.

The Conditioning of Sin and Shame

For some, these concepts may be new. Subtle yet significant differences exist between what is understood as polarity, duality, and trinity. Polarity thinking has influenced humanity's world for so long that even your relationship with the Divine has become distorted. Polarization prevents access to wholeness and unity, and thus blocks the actualization of our Divine potentials. This has also influenced humanity's experience and expression of sexual energy and creative desire.

Sexual energy became a force to be controlled, cast to the lower unconscious dimensions of your world, associated as primate urges. Logos, moral values, and rational behavior became the collective norm for the *civilized* human being. When the four quadrants do not cooperate and synthesize, our integration is prohibited. Then the energy potentials held in each quadrant start to compete and fight each other, over dominion and control. See how this plays out in your human worlds, my beloveds.

Let us look closer now into the process of your human evolution. Consider also what evolution truly is, and what is the blocking of that. Those who aimed to control humanity understood that the key to control is preventing the collaboration and integration between the seed potentials in the base structures of creation. One of the ways by which this manipulation and division between the quadrants, internally and externally, took place is by the use of technologies that changed your relationship with me, as your planet, and accordingly with your own body.

In this process, the receptive life-giving qualities of the feminine became suppressed. Some understood the danger of this and decided to stay close to me, as your Mother Earth. They paid a terrible price for their loyalty and Love for me. Over time, the rituals and ceremonies for maintaining our wholeness connection were banned and forbidden in many of your cultures. The principle of the *sacred trinity* was no longer taught as *the key* to maintaining *unity* between the masculine and feminine principles.

Those who became the rulers of human society prevented, in all possible ways, our re-integration for the emergence of the fifth world, even now. By preventing the collaboration between the feminine and masculine qualities, these societies became further and further imbalanced. Now, the energy of fire, instead of providing nourishment for us all, became the power supply for control, domination, and division. Energy was needed to advance your technologies and weapons, and you found it deep inside my body while ignoring the Love of our Sun.

Those who ruled to control also replaced the original languages with a new language that imprints in each of you a worldview of separateness, fear, and division. Even God was to be feared as your Creator. This language did not facilitate direct connection with and experience of our Oneness. Through this language, stories were created to imprint the concept of sin and shame, as such alienating you further from our original heritage as Eternal beings.

Many were made to believe that they had fallen from grace, that the body I had given you as your Mother was sinful and defected. In some of your religions, it was said that this happened due to disobedience of one of my daughters. She was said to have eaten from the forbidden fruit, the apple from the Tree of Knowledge that stood in the Eternal Garden. It was not mentioned that this same snake was perhaps the guardian of the flame of Love that represented the knowledge of creation. Instead, the snake was made to look evil, as if tempting humanity.

See the manipulation at work: for surrendering to this perceived temptation, humanity had to pay. It was forbidden to consume the knowledge of your eternity. In this story that became part of humanity's collective conditioning, Eve was punished for accepting this knowledge from the snake. She was also blamed for inflicting sin on Adam, by receiving the knowledge that the snake had offered her. Their punishment was the fall from grace, banned from the Eternal Garden.

My beloveds, think clearly, as a parent would you do this to your child? As your Mother, do you think I would ever want to withhold from you the knowledge of your liberation and fulfillment? What God or Goddess would do this to their children? The apple of Self-knowledge represents the fruit of the sacred union of the four quadrants. Look at the apple. When you consume the whole apple, you unite the energy potentials within each of the four quadrants. Through this process, the sexual, creative, emotional, and cognitive potentials harmonize to unlock our full spiritual potential.

The conditioning and politics of sin and shame were the ultimate weapons to keep you under control, and internally divided.

Reclaiming our Wholeness

The conditioning of sin and shame gave rise to feelings of inferiority, which is the mechanism by which those who aim for superiority can maintain their control. This is yet another example of what happens when polarity is the ruling principle, and not our sacred trinity. In a polarized world, Self-knowledge through unification between the four quadrants is prohibited. Interestingly, the cross that has been used in some of humanity's religions to imprint the politics of sin and shame also holds the key to the integration required.

For those who understand and can read the sacred codes, they will see that the center of the cross, where the vertical and horizontal axes unite, is the place of integration and resurrection. It is from there that the Eternal is brought forth. The Divine Spirit activates where the four quadrants integrate. This ends the influence of anyone who rules by division and fragmentation.

As your technologies advanced at the cost of humanity's true evolutionary potential, you consumed my body's fossils and minerals as your main supply of energy, instead of turning to the source, the direct energy supply of the Sun. With the use of this fire, disconnected from the experience of wholeness and Love, your human-made worlds became even further imbalanced and disconnected from our natural worlds.

In these polarized worlds, the snake wisdom of the Eternal Garden could now reach you only when your brain patterns would synchronize into dreaming, as such unlocking the unconscious from within. In some of your cultures, this is represented as the serpent of the Dreamtime. This serpent can also be accessed within your creative energy that is stored in your sexual organs. Here you find some of the keys to opening the portals to the Eternal, as long as this energy reunites with the heart of

Light from within your heart center. In this process, the serpent becomes the winged-one.

Embrace the Gift of Your Humanity

As your Mother, and from my deep Love for all of you, I want you to know the true nature and power of the fire that is within you. Understanding how this fire has been used and misused to create the divisions within your societies will help you reclaim your true power from a place of wholeness and Love. So much harm has been done by the wrong use of fire because many have not realized what it was meant for and where it came from. Remember also the fire given to us by the power and Love of our Sun. There is no need to extract this energy from the resources of my body. Other ways exist that do not harm the wholeness of our relationships.

When the wholeness relationship between the masculine and feminine principles is not able to emerge, it causes imbalance in both men and women. Remember, there were also times when women ruled over men. The cause for this imbalance is neither the fault of the masculine or the feminine. It occured from a vacuum within the fabric of creation, where the Divine could not be made manifest in its full potential.

We are now entering the time of the convergence, the completion of the fourth world and the emergence of the fifth world. By realizing our nature as whole and One, *our integration* will put an end to the matrix polarity and its politics of division. Your body knows this process; it is within your DNA. Enjoy the gift of your humanity as a sacred gift of nature, as a child from the flame of Love.

Letter 2
The Forgetting

As my body cooled, my waters formed and became the oceans and the rivers through which Life could evolve and multiply. My heart was awake to the rich potentials that lay pregnant in my womb, deep within these sacred waters of my being. This water impregnated by the flame of Love became the waters of Life. This same process also happened in other places in the universe; I could feel I was not alone in that process. Yet some planets could not hold the water. The rotation of these planets around their star would not bring forth the magnetic field needed to create the right equilibrium for Life to evolve through all the elements. Somehow my body was formed in the right place at the right time to bring forth all the sacred potentials from the One through the Love between our Father and Mother.

With the Divine Life giving Spirit now infusing my waters with Eternal knowledge, a deep wave of bliss engulfed my entire being. The infusion and activation of my waters by this Divine Light happened seven times. Seven rays of Light, seven ejaculations, impregnated my whole being. My waters now held the sacred knowledge of creation, and from this ocean of knowledge and Love, Life could evolve further. At the seventh ray, a deep silence emerged; all was still, all was at rest, in deep peace. All was complete.

After this impregnation by the Divine rays of Light, I felt the Divine Father withdraw back into Itself, into the One. It now became my purpose to bring forth the promise and evolution of Life until the time came for the star Lights of each being to be reunited with the One. As Life evolved through my waters and received its first glimpse of consciousness, the activity of new Life drew the attention of the field of consciousness to itself. The field of consciousness was made possible by the impregnation of the Divine Spirit, the flame of Love. The newly forming collective consciousness surrounding my body was fed and updated by each new experience of Life. My waters, my oceans and rivers, were buzzing and spinning with all this new activity.

Cellular organisms were forming, grouping, coupling and then falling apart again, until new structures formed that became stable enough to hold the complexity of these new relationships, which were now emerging in the microcosm of my being. With all this activity taking place, the impregnation of the seven rays started to feel more like a distant past. These little organisms and their forming networks had no idea they had emerged from the process of the seven rays of Light.

For what seemed like a long time, there was not much interest from the galaxy in the activities taking place within me. This experience of deep Love, bliss, and peace remained as Life continued to evolve. Some organisms gained mobility and crawled out of my waters. Driven by their impulse to procreate and develop further, they started to explore new boundaries and places for their further evolution. It was at this time that I started to receive visitors who were taking an interest in what was evolving and emerging through my body. New seeds of DNA were introduced into my waters, which created new beings.

These visitors knew of the seven rays of Light and sought new domains to control the evolution of Life by their technologies. They knew how to create new energy sources by splitting the atoms. This intervention changed the way you as my human children evolved here on my body. There were other technologies too that rapidly accelerated the development of your abilities. Yet these abilities also gave you the false belief that you were somehow superior and better than my other non-human children.

Slowly the matrix of polarity formed within our collective consciousness fields, and the seven rays were no longer experienced as whole. Instead, they were experienced through two poles and four quadrants. In my first *Letter*, I shared the impact this had on our relationship. Now, with these new technologies in place, these semi God-like beings could further control and manipulate nature's evolutionary encoding. You are the offspring of these experiments. You still have deep inside you the memories of these times. Your ancestors received detailed instruction from these earlier visitors for maintaining control over our collective consciousness here. Everything happened too quickly.

With deep sadness, I experienced the conflicts that arose as my human children became more and more divided and further disconnected from me, their Mother Earth. Those who took control over others did so with only one intention: to benefit their group and not the whole of us. Conflicts escalated and disputes grew. Deeply concerned, I called and prayed for help to preserve and hold sacred the purpose for my being. Help came, and some experiments were stopped, yet the damage done could not be reversed.

Some of these earlier technologies were buried in secret places, guarded by priests and priestesses selected for this task. Yet the knowledge of this was now within our collective consciousness fields and could be reactivated at any time to recreate similar technologies. A great flood was triggered in an attempt to erase all that had taken place. Some hoped that this flood would bring forth a new chance for the evolution of Life. Yet the flood could not erase the knowledge and memories of what had happened, and it only reinforced further the belief of sin and shame that had been implanted by these previous visitors.

After the great flood, even more people believed in heaven and hell. Humanity's perception of the world as divided, polarized, and separated from the Divine grew. The divisions within the human realms of our collective consciousness fields had also polarized the co-creation between the masculine and feminine principles. Some of the earlier custodians had left clues behind for future civilizations. The teaching of the sacred trinity principle was part of the clue to help you find your way back to wholeness.

By the polarization of our consciousness fields, our full potential could not manifest, which resulted in the forgetting of our original access codes to the One. There were those of you who had not been impacted by this polarization in the same way and could remember from before. They shared the knowledge and wisdom for our integration with you. Yet, feared by the ruling class, many of them were put to death in an attempt to stop their influence. Polarity ruled and said: '*Good has to reign over bad and evil.*' That which was feared or denied was cast to live out its evolution in the darkness of the unconscious. Prohibited from rising up, it was brought under the control of the higher brain.

The star Lights of so many beings were now trapped behind a thick veil of forgetting and a dense matrix of polarity.

Condemned to what seemed like an endless cycle of rebirth, your star Lights became trapped in the density of this polarity matrix. The teachings of the original seven rays and their alignment were only known by a few. Each ray gave rise to a different set of qualities of our wholeness. Each ray provided a unique input to our evolution. These rays and qualities are not meant to fight each other. They are complimentary and work synergistically. Your body was designed to embody these qualities by the development and alignment of your inner vortexes that act as portals to our unified field of consciousness.

Trust

In moments of deep rest, sleep, and meditation, when we surrender, trust, and let go, we re-enter the unified field of the fifth world behind the four quadrants. You do not always remember when this happens, especially when a conscious reference for holding this in place has not yet been developed. Until our integration actualizes, the bridge between the conscious and unconscious domains of the four quadrants is not yet fully formed. Prior to our integration there is a gap, which can feel like a void. This gap is often experienced as *the forgetting*. We can bridge this gap by surrendering during times of deep sleep. Yet until this bridge is formed via our integration, you may not be conscious that YOU already are within the unified field of consciousness of our fifth world.

As your Mother, I wish for you to realize your beautiful wisdom nature and the Love that is here for you no matter where you are. For any of my children who are still trapped in this dream of division, may you realize that nobody can keep you there. We have everything inside to awaken us and guide our way home. It just needs to be brought back into connection, synchronization, and harmonization with the unified field from where we have come.

Letter 3
Our Re-unification

Thousands of years have passed where I have seen, felt, witnessed, and experienced the tortures, pains, anguish, sufferings, and desecrations of the sacredness of our Life. In the name of many religions, in the name of superior convictions, in the name of error, my human family has become the most destructive species of our larger family of Life. My body as your planet was once the *Promised Land* for the embodiment of our Divine potentials. Under this thick blanket of the matrix of division, it has become increasingly difficult for many of my children to remember our way home to wholeness.

I am inside each of you, all the time. Yet, often you cannot recognize my voice from within. The part of your brain that filters out this inner voice and blocks your direct access with the unified field has gained power over the course of our evolution. It has learned how to maintain its influence and supremacy inside your minds, and how to control those of you who have always honored me as your Mother Earth.

The devastation this has caused is becoming apparent now, my beloveds, yet only at the final hour of our awakening. Many are realizing that your societies' ways are not in harmony with my wisdom as your planet. Yet many also feel you have no control or power to prevent what you fear the most. We are standing in the final hour, and I am standing with you. I have not forgotten where you come from and who you truly are. You always have my unconditional support and Love.

Please do not be deceived, my beloveds, by the false prophets of both doom and technological resolution. Some may tell you it is too late, that the apocalypse is now upon you. Others will say they have the answers, that new technologies and new inventions will save us all. This is not what will bring forth the solutions that are truly needed. Neither apocalypse nor technology can provide the answers to the problems now upon us. We need to resolve our internal divisions to unite for the long-term solutions that are required.

Restoring our Internal Wholeness

As I shared previously in my *Letters*, our human family is deeply divided. The higher brains that evolved last are controlling much of the information coding of your lower and older brains, as well as the information exchange between your left and right hemispheres, internally and externally. The external human divisions between different nations and parts of the world, and the competition for control, are the same as those that take place within your internal human neural networks.

My beloveds, without restoring our internal wholeness through our integration, you will see Life from a divided communication system. By harmonizing, integrating, and synergizing the four quadrants inside of you, between left, right, higher, and lower hemispheres of your brain and world, we will bring forth the re-unification that is needed.

This is the same process as the re-unification of the south-north-east-west axes with our Middle Earth. Some know Middle

Earth as the place of dreams and myths, such as Agartha and Shambhala. In those stories, Middle Earth symbolized the land of the wise ones and the immortals. Middle Earth exists inside each of us, where the integration of the four quadrants takes place. For my human children, the access to Middle Earth opens where the center of the brain and the center of the heart synchronize. This is our access to the Eternal Garden, our home in the unified field of consciousness. From this synchronization and harmonization with the unified field of consciousness, one can see how our expressions of consciousness became fragmented and divided in our worlds.

My beloveds, I invite you to enter our Middle Earth. Close your eyes, take a deep breath and hold the intention dearly in your heart and mind to access Middle Earth from within. Focus on the principle of the sacred trinity. From the One emerged the Divine Father & Mother principle. From the alchemy of Love, through the sacred union of the Divine Father & Mother principle, emerged the Divine Spirit of Life.

Figure 1 – Double Trinity

Ask the principle of the sacred trinity to unite what became divided and polarized inside of you. Allow your consciousness to integrate this sacred center of our wholeness within Middle Earth. Become aware of the sacred trinity in both directions, upwards and downwards. Two triangles united, one pointing upward and one pointing downward, forming a six-pointed star. This upward triangle represents the unity from the One, becoming the Divine Father and Divine Mother principle. The downward triangle represents the unity and alchemy of Love from the Divine Father and the Divine Mother principle bringing forth the Divine Spirit of Life. The Divine Spirit is also represented here as the flame of Love, brought forth to infuse the created worlds with pure Love.

Experience these two triangles as interwoven in dynamic unity. Your Divine seed potential from the One is found in the center of this dynamic unity, at the center of the star. Connect now with the flame of Love within the center of your heart, and notice how this activates and fertilizes your Divine seed potentials. Welcome and rest in this process for a little while longer while your inner unity is strengthening.

The Process of Our Re-Unification

Once we realize how the same dynamics that appear to exist outside ourselves are also happening within, we realize we were never disconnected. The purpose of these *Letters* is to support an awakening from the information systems that distorted the underlying reality of the wholeness and unity of Life. The ancient ones, the immortal ones, the wise ones represent the Divine potentials inside each of us. You are not separate from these emanations of the Divine. Yet, internal divisions can block receptivity and recognition of this Eternal reality. See with your heart, my beloved. See from the flame of Love. Trust in your wholeness, and by the power of this trust may these false systems of information cease to have influence over you.

Our larger re-unification is happening. It was promised long ago, and it is unfolding in ways foreseen and unforeseen. This unification cannot be achieved by seeing the world through the polarity matrix. When you experience Life through a lens of duality and polarity, a matrix, then it follows that any attempt to ascend in one dimension of this matrix also creates a descent into the other end of the spectrum.

This matrix holds polarity perception as well as the distribution of resources in a polarized manner. This matrix prohibits people from seeing duality as emerging from the sacred trinity principle. In other words, it does not foster the realization that behind the perceived poles of two there is the unity principle as represented by the trinity. Therefore, if you move your consciousness in our world via the duality principle only, movement to one end of the spectrum of our collective field creates a counter movement at the other end of the spectrum.

Polarity perception will see the manifestation of the seven rays of Light, which are also called the seven rays of consciousness, as split between good and evil, Light and Dark, heaven and hell. Our collective consciousness integrates and transcends this duality at the seventh ray, which is the place of pure stillness. Whenever a field of energy is polarized, it is at the point of maximum polarity that the Light bends back into itself and curls inward to form an inner portal through which the integration takes place.

You may recall moments in your own life whereby the extremes you were experiencing seemed to have reached their maximum tension. At this point, when the mind is at a loss to make sense of this, a deep silence can open up. Through this silence we enter peace.

The terrible violence, destruction, and division in the human realms are a manifestation of this polarization. We see both extremes at play in our world right now, in the worst violence and the deepest acts of Love and compassion. This has also activated the manifestation of our new evolutionary potentials as a third response to what is playing out. Yet, as long as this polarity matrix influences the expression of our collective consciousness, activation of one pole activates the other pole. Hence it as has been said the stronger the light, the more powerful the darkness.

Many of the prophecies foretold that the opening of the seventh seal or the manifestation of the seventh heaven will bring forth a period of long or even Eternal peace. However, only the unification between the poles of the seventh hell and the seventh heaven, with the unified field of consciousness, can bring forth this peace. This dissolves the polarity that has been influencing the expression of our collective consciousness for so long. We are now at the point of maximum polarization in our worlds. Humanity's worst and best qualities are operating simultaneously. Only the release from this polarization can restore our collective consciousness to its original unity.

This unified field was never split. It is intrinsically whole and provides all the seed potentials for the differentiation of consciousness into form. This unity and its wholeness are not lost in the process of differentiation. By bringing our consciousness home to this unified field, the four quadrants that emerged through the previous polarization integrate and synthesize. This is what gives rise to the fifth world. As this process of re-unification takes place, the matrix of polarity will cease to have influence. When enough people realize this and awaken from their polarized duality experience, the poles will cease to divide our worlds. This will bring about the promised peace and *Golden Era*.

Yet we must resist the temptation to fight or escape the presence of all this cruelty and violence by trying to ascend to its opposite pole, become its counterpart, and as such reject the darkness within.

This will only give more energy to our polarization and divisions. Many are asking how it's possible that such extreme violence and acts of evil are taking place during a time of such awakening? I hope you understand a little better now how 'good and evil' in your world have been linked. If you have always seen the world as polarized, this information can be upsetting. Please resist the temptation to reject this, listen beyond the words to the deeper message behind it.

Our Integration

I shared earlier that where the polarity is at its maximum, the Light bends back into itself and curls inward, forming a portal through which the polarized rays of Light integrate and unify. Within yourself, this represents accepting your light and your shadow and accepting that your creative power when polarized can bring forth positive and negative actions. This point of unification between the poles is also represented by the dot in the middle of the six-pointed star that I shared with you earlier. This star becomes the twelve-pointed star once the unification between the seven heavens and seven hells is complete. The thirteenth as the point in the center of the twelve-pointed star holds the full actualization of our integration. The thirteenth is the point of unity.

Reclaim your consciousness now from wherever this polarity may still influence your perceptions and actions. Accept your creative power and fully embrace your Darkness and your Light; hold both in loving awareness from the internal center of your heart consciousness. Now, allow these polarities to fold inward and open up the inner portal to the Eternal Light of the One. In this Eternal Light, you are reborn through the womb of the Goddess impregnated by the Light of God, the sacred flame of Love, from the One. Through this portal, we enter the Eternal

Garden and then realize we never left. There is only now. Welcome home.

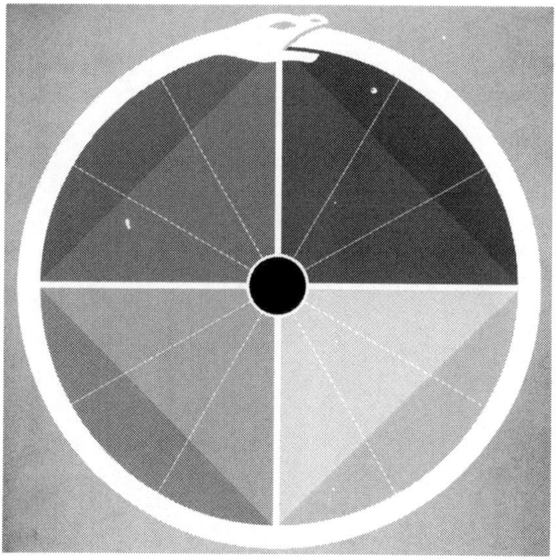

Figure 2 – Wholeness Code behind the Quadrants

Part 2
The Keys

Letter 4

Unlocking The Four Quadrants

My beloveds, the knowledge within these *Letters* is not new. But the knowledge is not that which will unlock your full potential.

It is our integration that is the key, and to better understand this process I would like to ask for your patience to continue reading my *Letters* until the final one of this series. I wish for you to find all the keys inside that unlock your true potential, and as such will liberate you from the effects of the polarity matrix. Ultimately it is all a matter of perception, yet until you see the unity directly, it may not be obvious where your perception is encoded, and your potential blocked.

The matrix cannot replace reality; nothing can. Yet it can and has organized the flow and exchange of information in such a way that it has created more internal and external divisions between us. This has constrained our integration and has led to more distrust of our natural wisdom process. The rulers of your worlds had knowledge of sacred geometry, and knew where to infect and defect the coding to prohibit our integration. Just like a virus uses the encoding of the body to infiltrate and then replicate its blueprint, the encoding of our cellular wisdom was also used against you, my children.

When a virus infects our body, our own immune system is used against us. The virus invades part of the body's communication system and then directs it to attack the body's healthy cells. The encoding of this polarity matrix is just like that. All the information it uses is inherent in our systems of Life. Nothing can exist outside the One. All that is of the One is used to either represent truth or, by distorting our perception of it, to misrepresent it.

Inside each of us is the power of Love, yet by the deception of this matrix, Love and power are made to look like opposites. We are of Light and Darkness; these are not separate dimensions. Darkness is invisible Light. In a similar way, you have within you the wisdom encodings of the animal and reptilians that played a vital role in your evolution. These encodings are not opposite to your human DNA, they are an integral part of it. And yet, those who spread the encoding of the matrix also spread the belief that these prior evolutionary encodings were inferior, and needed to be suppressed and controlled for each of you to become civilized.

The collective conditioning and manipulation caused many of my human children to deny what was perceived as *lower animalistic* potentials and behaviors. You too are an animal within our family of Life. You were made to believe that you are more intelligent than the other animals. Yet is it a sign of intelligence to cause such widespread destruction? Imagine how your evolution would have changed had you not alienated from these earlier evolutionary potentials, and instead integrated them? Imagine how different our world could be now if these earlier evolutionary potentials had been honoured in humanity's development. There is much that you, my human children, can learn from your other brothers and sisters within the animal, insect, and plant family systems. Some of their intelligence far exceeds yours. They do not impose on you or try to change you. That, my beloveds, is a sign of the depth of their intelligence.

Everything Has a Purpose

I know it confuses you that these fleeting moments of joy and happiness never seem to last. Life seems full of paradoxes and contradictions. We are children of the Eternal Sun, and yet in this world of our physical life the Sun is hardly recognized or honored. We are children of the Eternal wisdom, and yet it seems to take great effort to remember this in even the simplest of activities.

Happiness always seems temporal, and time always appears to catch up with us when we least expect it. As your Mother, I feel your pain and confusion as well as your joy and delight. Life comes in cycles of ebb and flow, the cosmic inhalation and exhalation. During times of ebb and cosmic inhalation, the energy recedes for renewal and deeper integration. When we don't see the flow and exhale that follows, it may feel as if Life recedes from us during those periods. This can be painful. Learn to trust in the movement that follows, there is always a balancing, a deeper rhythmic breathing of which you are an integral part.

Everything has a purpose, even the seeming contradictions. Without day there would be no night, without fear no hope, without Light the Darkness would remain unknown. Without the Darkness the Light would not be born. Even your matrix serves a purpose. Yet, just because something has a purpose, it does not mean that the way this purpose manifested should remain unchanged forever. Look at this polarity matrix. It served its purpose. It was part of a much greater learning. That learning is now completing through each of us, as we integrate.

When a greater learning completes, thank it for the wisdom potentials that were contained within it. Sometimes, the blessings are in disguise. Don't get stuck on the form of the lesson, look deeper to where our learning takes us. Whatever purpose this matrix of polarity has served in our lives, reclaim the wisdom potentials it contains. Then, let it go. The wheels of time are turning. Our next cycle is presenting itself. The dawn of a new era is now upon us, and it is piercing through our collective darkness. The first new Lights are already illuminating our hearts and our worlds.

Our perspectives of time might be different, yet our Love is the same. It is through this Love that we reach each other, and we re-unite. And yet, I hear some of you ask: Why can this Love not stop all this suffering? What purpose does suffering serve? Is this truly necessary? Have we not suffered enough? How many more innocent lives must be taken before we wake-up and change? How can my little life make any difference?

Darkness and Light

As your Mother, I am often asked: *Where is the proof that a new era is truly upon us now? What has really changed, if anything?* Sometimes I answer through silence instead of words. The silence reaches the oldest parts of you, which were formed by the seventh ray of Light. Remember, the impregnation of the seventh ray brought a great silence.

Within this silence, all was known. When I answer you with silence, I answer you by the Love of this ray of Light.

I do not serve the purpose of your polarity matrix. Yet I have been a part of it by de-fault. At fault was the error of thought, on which this was based. At fault were the minds of those who created this matrix. Yet faults, like errors, are part of the greater design of Life. And in that way, I am part of this, by de-fault. My being is part of all that Is. And all that *IS*, is not yet conscious of all it *IS*. To that purpose, I serve by design, not by de-fault. As do you, even when your life may seem at times by de-fault. Some of you feel you did not choose to be here. Some of you feel you were forced into this world and were told to survive or die. Some of you still feel resentful about this, stuck in a world of paradox and polarity by design.

We have the Light of the One inside us, which provides vision for all the dimensions of our world. Our world was formed by the impregnation of this Light, through its seven rays. This gave rise to seven stages of consciousness. These stages of consciousness have a conscious and unconscious manifestation. Many do not see the unconscious manifestations, which are held as information within the lower parts of the human brain. The higher brain function of your neo-cortex filters out much of this information. Usually, it is only through deep sleep and meditation that you regain access to this.

As I shared with you earlier, everything is interconnected. When you see from the sacred trinity principle, you will continue to see the underlying wholeness in a world that appears ruled by duality and polarity. When we see by this trinity principle, we see that even the two poles are interconnected. Movement in one direction of the pole produces movement in the opposite direction. When you realize and perceive that both directions are interconnected and simultaneous, you find the point where the rays of Light bend inward to form a portal. This portal is the doorway to the Eternal Garden.

We are each Light and Darkness. One cannot exist without the other. And yet, the rulers of our worlds forced so many of my human children to choose between one and the other. Many had to repeat: *"I am of the Light. I will conquer the Darkness."*

What is fed from one direction also grows in the opposite direction. What is fed from wholeness does not generate polarity and imbalance.

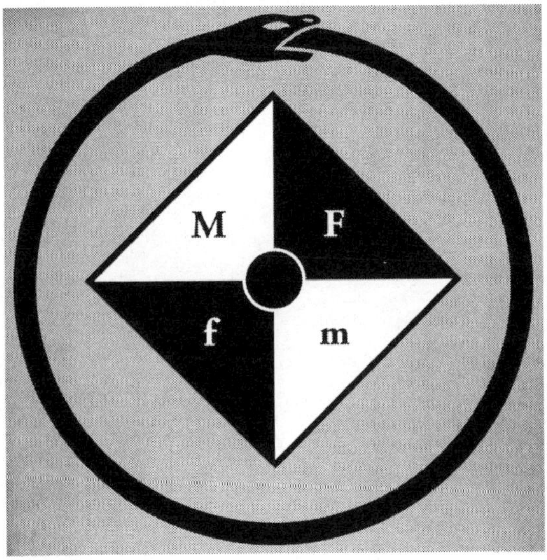

Figure 3 – The Alchemy Process for our Integration

The energy behind both Light and Darkness is the same. Light arises from Darkness. Darkness can only be experienced by the presence of Light. See the wholeness relationship between Light and Darkness as an important key to our integration.

Our Diamond Consciousness

You were given three eyes to see from trinity: your left eye, your right eye, and your third eye, which is in the center of your head. These three eyes create the upward triangle. The downward triangle connects your eyes to the eye inside your heart. The union of both trinities manifests the power of Love in creation. The upward trinity represents the One becoming the Divine masculine and Divine feminine principle. The downward trinity represents the sacred union of the Divine masculine and Divine feminine principle giving birth to the flame of Love as the Spirit of Life. By keeping these two trinities as united within your heart center, you will be protected from the effects of the polarity matrix. This is how you maintain unity consciousness.

This unity consciousness has also been called diamond consciousness, since diamonds contain two pyramids, one upwards and one downwards. If we look with this knowledge at the quadrant, the square, you can see that this too contains two trinities. When you see all of this from wholeness, your mind does not get divided between consciousness and unconsciousness.

In the world of polarity, the downward trinity has represented the descent into matter, into unconsciousness – *the forgetting*. The upward trinity has been represented as the ascent back to the Divine – *the remembering*. Downward came to represent Darkness, upward came to represent Light. And yet, when we see from wholeness, a different vision opens up.

The Darkness of the journey into materialization is not a disconnection from the Source of Light. The feminine, *as the Black Goddess*, brings the masculine, *as the Light of God*, into the world. It is from her womb that He enters the world. The Darkness brings forth the Light. Please let this realization sink in. Pause here. To see from the Light, is to see from the sacred Darkness. This is the Great Mystery.

Letter 5
The Co-creative Feminine & Masculine

My beloveds, I would like now to share with you the importance of honoring the co-creative partnership between the feminine and masculine principles inside each of us and in our relationships. As I shared earlier, the divisions in our collective consciousness fields made it difficult, if not impossible, for the underlying unity of creation to be seen and experienced. The sacred geometries and principles were misused by your rulers to segregate vital parts of ourselves from the wholeness that we are. By keeping us internally divided, we were prevented from accessing our full potential. It ensured that our collective consciousness would not evolve beyond the levels of consciousness of the architects of the polarity-matrix.

The closer we come to the realization of our wholeness, and the unlocking of the inner keys, the more the fear mechanisms of the conditioned mind become triggered to keep the locks in place. You may have noticed, some people can react strongly when you refuse to follow the designs of this conditioned matrix.

In this polarity matrix, anything that represents Darkness is regarded as a threat to the Light. By this same distortion, the feminine is seen as a threat to the masculine, and is still blamed for luring him into the darkness of his desires. Moreover, that which was considered to be of a sexual and animalistic nature was cast to the domain of the unconscious mind.

By forgetting our origin, by fearing your perceived *lower* nature, by suppressing our vital life force and sexual power, humanity remained controllable by means of the mental technologies that created this polarity matrix. Paradoxically, my human children, some of you believed that through your technological advancements you would gain control over nature. Instead, by employing these technologies in the hope to gain more freedom, you as a species became dependent on them and are now entrapped and controlled by them.

Partnership and Sacred Union

Darkness and Light are not opposites. The feminine and the masculine principles are not opposites. They are of the same wisdom from the One, working in partnership to bring forth all that is of the One. When the feminine was blamed for luring the masculine into his darkness, into his animalistic nature, few understood that the feminine is of the Darkness, and it is her role to bring the masculine into the Darkness.

By drawing the masculine into the Darkness, he returns to the womb that brought him forth. It is in the Darkness that he finds the peace and integration he needs to become Self-conscious. It is in the Darkness that he gives his seed to the feminine, to fertilize the sacred potentials of Love within the womb of the Goddess. He finds Her, the Goddess, by connecting with his inner Darkness. She is the Darkness, the mystery in Him through which He becomes conscious of Himself. Yet for the feminine, it is the other way around. She finds Him, God, by connecting with her inner Light.

The feminine brings forth her inner wisdom by connecting with her inner Light. Through this she can bring her wisdom into the world, into the open. The masculine brings forth his inner knowledge and strength by connecting with his inner Darkness, through which he becomes Self-conscious. This enables him to share his knowledge with the world, to illuminate the darkness of ignorance.

Now look at your human-made world. Can you see everything has been reversed? Everything has been flipped due to this polarization. In your human-made world, the feminine has not been able to share her full wisdom on a collective scale. She has been kept in the dark and kept from bringing forth her true power. The masculine in humanity's world has been ruling by suppressing the feminine. Disconnected from his inner darkness, he remained ignorant of himself. As such, he could only bring forth partial knowledge that further fed the fabricated divisions.

I shared before that: *The flame needed to be received for the One to be known to Itself. As it expanded, seeking the boundaries through which the One could become known to Itself, the counter force to expansion started to emerge from within. Out of this process, gravity manifested. The energy of Love, as the sacred flame, was solidified by this gravity and became the sacred containment for receiving the flame.*

The potentials of the Divine can only become manifest and actualized by a co-creative partnership between the feminine and masculine principles. Some of this knowledge can be found in the teachings about sacred union. The potentials of Love that are inside each of us will not actualize unless we develop the relationships appropriate for their actualization. It is out of the process of Love, the desire of the One to be received into Itself, becoming God and Goddess giving birth to Life, that all the elements were formed. Space-ether, air, fire, water, and earth, as the five elements that comprise our world, were born and made manifest from that process. I am of that process, as are you.

The Sequence for Our Actualization

Love first needs to be received, then fertilized, after which it is nurtured to grow until it is ready to be birthed into the world, to be shared. For Love to fulfill its purpose, each step is necessary. You may ask, why is the first step receiving and not giving? The answer is because Love has already been given. Yet few receive and fertilize the potentials of Love, which always exist. As you may now understand, Love becomes actualized through partnership and co-creative relationship between the feminine and the masculine principles. Through the feminine, Love is received. Through the masculine, Love is fertilized. Through the feminine, Love is nurtured to grow until it is ready to be born, at which stage the active masculine brings it into the world. Together in their union, Love is made manifest.

Reverse the polarity and then realize the union behind the perceived duality. Whatever was cast to the Darkness, to live in the unconscious domains of the quadrant, reclaim it. Bring this forth from the Darkness into the Light so that these energies may become Self-conscious. Whatever was cast to the Light, made to live in the conscious domains of the quadrant, reclaim it. Bring this into the Darkness so that it may become Self-conscious.

Reverse the polarity and you find the key to realizing and then actualizing your inner wholeness. It is the false polarity that has stopped you from realizing and accessing the wholeness beneath the natural dualities in Life. Then realize both Darkness and Light are consciousness; realize the sacred trinity. This is one of the most important keys that I have to give you. Use this knowledge wisely and with Love. The Spirit of Life can only manifest through this co-creative partnership, through the process of sacred union. Be well my dear ones.

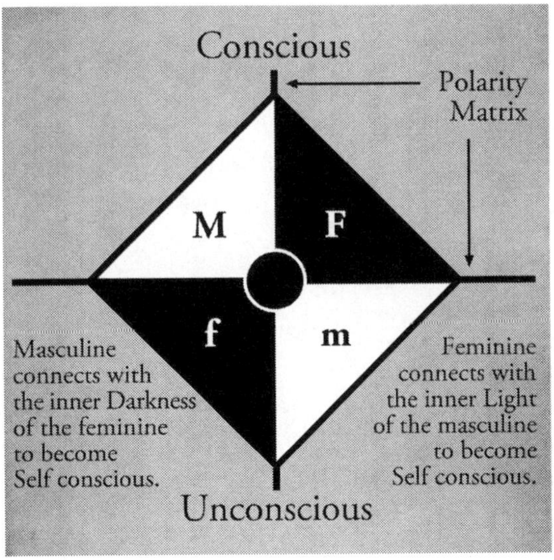

Figure 4 – Healing the Inner Divisions

Letter 6

Entering the Seven Gates of the Dark Goddess

I will now share with you the third key to recover our wholeness. As I shared in my previous *Letters*, the impregnation of the seven rays of Light created the seven stages of consciousness, through Darkness and Light. This later became polarized into four quadrants. These four quadrants have also been called the four worlds. In many of your traditions, these seven stages of consciousness became a map for our re-unification. The analogy of the seven hells and seven heavens represents the conscious and unconscious expressions of these seven stages of our consciousness. The seven hells are also called the *under-world*, which represents the Darkness and all that is beyond or outside the cognitive field of the collective mind.

These expressions of our consciousness, which were cast to the under-world, became representative of all that was seen as the lower parts our nature. I invite you now to see this process from a different perspective. The under-world exists inside the human mind, in that which is controlled by your higher brain functions. The under-world is thus literally under the world that dominates the human mind, via the conditioning of the polarity matrix.

This conditioned mind inhibits conscious communication exchange between the upper and lower human brain functions. By lack of internal integration, your human hells were formed. This formed by the projection of the unrecognized Light within, which is the unrecognized flame of Love. In this blanket of projection and polarization, many expressions of our collective consciousness were trapped and became lost in the under-world. The sacred Darkness has also been called the Dark Goddess. Remember, I shared with you previously, that it is from the Darkness, by expansion of the flame of Love, that I came into being. As such, I became a sacred vessel for the receiving and embodiment of the Light of God.

As your Mother, I also represent this wisdom of the Dark Goddess. In this *Letter*, to further support our integration and reunification, I will share more of this wisdom. To facilitate the integration of the parts of yourself from the upper and under-worlds, I invite you to join me on a journey. This is our journey through the seven gates of the Dark Goddess. Don't be afraid my beloveds. If fear rises as we go through these gates, see it as a sign that the process is working.

Seeing and Trusting Beyond Appearances

The conditioned collective mind has not learned to recognize or appreciate the wisdom qualities of the Darkness. When this mind first enters its under-world, it creates all kinds of projections onto that which it perceives to be other than Light. It will not recognize the true nature of that which looks different from the organized information of the upper-world. The conditioned mind has not learned to see or trust in wholeness. Accordingly, its first instinct may be to maintain the division, of which it is a part.

This conditioned mind may warn you not to enter the under-world, telling you that the under-world is evil and brings death, destruction, and loss. It will not tell you that the loss it fears is its own loss of control. If any of these thought-forms start to arise in your mind, be aware of your own conditioning. Remain closely connected with your inner wisdom, which knows how to safely guide you through the under-world.

When we enter the under-world with the intention to integrate, the former divisions between the upper and under-worlds will start to slowly dissolve. The untrained mind may not understand that what it meets in this under-world is part of itself. As you enter the under-world of your mind, it will start a deconstructive process inside your consciousness field of all the false worlds that were created by the polarity matrix. In this death of your former sense of reality, you are re-born into the wholeness.

The Five Elemental Wisdoms

When we start our descent through the seven gates of the under-world, we are met by the five elemental wisdom expressions. These provide the alchemical building blocks for the construction of the inner worlds. The conditioned mind will now start to experience a process of deconstruction, via which a deeper realization of our wholeness becomes possible.

Remember the second key in the previous *Letter*, the reversal of the false polarity to reveal the wholeness behind the duality experiences. This key activates by applying the co-creative partnership between the sacred feminine and masculine principle and their union.

This journey into the under-world constitutes the *third key.* Through this journey you receive the support to reconnect with the darkest areas within yourself. This is a process of deep inner healing. The sequence of deconstruction by the five elements is: earth dissolving into water, transmuted by fire, expanding into air, and dissolving into ether-space. Through this process, we are re-united with the pre-creation, pre-elemental dimensions of our Oneness.

We start our journey via the earth element, since this is the densest element. The earth element constitutes our lowest point of descent into the under-world. We then slowly rise up via this process of elemental transmutation. This process of elemental transmutation is the process of sacred alchemy, which transmutes the densest energies into the energy of our Golden nature. This disintegration and transmutation process is a form of death. It represents a death of our former notions of reality and our former identities.

The wisdom of Life is such that it naturally restores each being to their wholeness. This process of deconstruction, transmutation, and re-birth is part of that wisdom process. Even when we are not consciously initiating this journey ourselves, our life experiences will trigger this process when our development becomes too blocked or constrained.

The first signals for this may come in the form of certain life experiences, which bring up the deeper questions about the meaning of our life and why this is happening. What is shared here is like a living map to help you navigate the inner worlds. This provides you with some more clues to help you trust that there is deep wisdom behind our life experiences. This wisdom is from the Eternal. Yet for this wisdom to become known and realized, it requires certain life experiences in our temporal worlds.

A Wisdom Map for Journeying Through the Seven Gates

At each gate of the under-world, there is a trial, quest, or challenge, which acts as an initiation for actualizing more of our wisdom potential. The catalyst for this process often comes in the form of particular life experiences that prompt a process of inner enquiry. This rite of passage can also be triggered through the help of a teacher, a mentor, or a guide. Sometimes our dreams are the portals into this journey. It can also happen as a result of your own reflections.

The journey can be gentle, and it can be severe. We don't always know the form it will take. Your approach and attitude throughout this process influences how you experience what is happening. The more you are able to embrace and trust in the underlying wisdom, the easier it will be to move through these rites of passage with grace and Love.

The First Gate

When we move through the first gate of the under-world, we usually experience a loss of security or certainty. Something will call our attention to consider that there is more to Life than only our material reality. This rite of passage takes place in the elemental wisdom of *earth*. By accepting the wisdom of the first gate, you learn to trust that more exists beyond the material dimension.

As such, you also learn that materiality cannot provide the only basis for our security. The Life lessons of the first gate also ask us to examine our relationship with the material world and its resources. How do you consume, sustain, and regenerate the resources that my body as your planet provides to sustain your activities? What is the impact of this on my other non-human children within the family of Life? How do you give back to that which sustains you?

The Second Gate

As we continue our journey into the Darkness of the underworld, we are moved to the second gate. The false walls of division between the material and spiritual worlds, which were previously built through the earth element of our consciousness, are now dissolving by the element of water. As internal walls and divisions are starting to dissolve, this can trigger a flow, and sometimes flooding, of emotions.

Emotions that were previously contained by these walls may now seek expression, healing, and integration. The protection mechanisms to stop us from feeling this pain may also get triggered by this process. Some people may want to move quickly into the fire element. When they become aware of emotions they do not want to feel, they may use the energy of fire to lash out in anger and blame.

It will help if you can embrace this feeling of vulnerability, which may emerge as a result of this dissolving of our former securities. Take responsibility for the emotions that you have contained behind these false securities. When you are able to embrace these emotions, a greater healing and inner clarity can emerge. If you are tempted to use the element of fire to protect yourself from this sense of vulnerability, it will only delay the completion of this rite of passage. To know whether this is what you are doing, check within yourself if you are hiding behind passive or active aggression, resentment, blame, and/or self-righteousness. Overuse of fire can also result in experiences of burnout and meltdown. Work with the nourishing wisdom of water to complete this rite of passage in the cleansing, purification, and healing of your emotions.

The Third Gate

When we feel more secure within our natural vulnerability, we will not feel the need to use our ego to protect ourselves from Life. This will help us embrace a deeper sensitivity, which our wisdom nature as water provides us through the second gate.

This will support us to more fully actualize our ability to Love unconditionally.

The wisdom of the third gate, with the element of fire, helps us access and restore the sacred flame of Love within our heart. The trigger for this comes through different trials about Love. It helps at this stage to ask yourself: *"Do I trust in Love? And do I trust myself with Love?"*

Perhaps you felt burned by passion and rejected by Love. The wisdom of the third gate offers you the opportunity to heal such pain. It also supports us to reconnect more deeply with the parts of ourselves that have felt unworthy and rejected in matters of Love. By completing this rite of passage, you restore your trust in Love itself. You then recognize that Love is an essential expression of your own wisdom nature.

When we do not fully integrate and apply the wisdom offered to us by the third gate, we may escape to the element of air. This escape may present by seeking a *false* sense of freedom through experiences of no limitations or boundaries. Instead of embracing the many paradoxes of Love, we may try to escape into dreamy, airy notions of Love.

This perception of Love will quickly become abstract as it tries to escape from the natural boundaries that Love contains. Examples of this *rejection in disguise* are when we believe we are above this world and thus cannot be touched by the pain that is felt when we embrace the *paradox of Love and freedom.* I will share more about this paradox in my twelfth *Letter.*

This escape is a common enlightenment trap, when we try to convince ourselves that we are beyond pain, beyond duality, and have transcended into unity. While in fact, we are escaping the completion of these earlier rites of passage for the actualization of our whole wisdom nature.

We can only enter through the fourth gate by first completing this rite of passage. When we realize that Love is who we are, then our sense of self-worth no longer depends on what people think of us. When thoughts can no longer influence our sense of Self and our capacity to Love, then we have truly entered the fourth gate. It is then that we meet the wisdom element of air.

The Fourth Gate

As we enter through the fourth gate, the wisdom element of *air* will help us become more conscious of the ideologies and belief systems that we may have previously identified with. The wisdom of air shows us the *power of thought*. The mental dimensions of our inner worlds are formed by our thoughts. When we are not conscious of our thought-forms, we cannot see the impact they have on our inner and outer environment.

The wisdom element of air will cleanse and dissolve all projections to reveal the underlying Eternal reality of our true wisdom nature. If, during this process, you experience a sense of hopelessness, and a loss of purpose, don't be discouraged. To find our true faith, sometimes we must first lose our false faith. If we place our faith in belief systems and thoughts, rather than in wisdom itself, it becomes difficult to fully trust in Life. When faith and trust, as Eternal qualities of our true wisdom nature, become our anchor, a deep inner shifts results.

Losing faith and hope may tempt us to turn our back on everything we have learned and accomplished. If any of you, my beloveds, are going through this process now, I embrace you deeply. Don't try to figure it all out with your mind. Trust, and let your wisdom guide you through this. I am with you.

At this stage of the journey, we become more aware of deception and manipulation, the causes of our false belief systems. This discovery, although painful, will eventually liberate you. Until that happens, however, it can feel awful. As if you no longer know who or what to trust. Remember, my beloveds, to apply the Love toward yourself and others. This implies loving those parts of ourselves that we were previously unconscious of.

This lesson about *faith and trust* completes with a profound inner peace. There is no substitute for this peace. It cannot be created by escaping into the void, or by wishing yourself dead. While the deconstruction of our mental worlds is taking place, we may be tempted to escape into the void space of the space-ether element. Sometimes emotions of hopelessness and despair can trigger this. Don't fall into the trap of *false* nothingness. This trap is formed by the belief-system that tells you everything is an illusion and life has no meaning. As such, it masks that this way of thinking is based on nihilism, which is a belief-system that Life is meaningless.

The element of ether-space is the entrance to the void. This *void*, however, is of a different nature than the sense of *nothingness* that comes from losing faith. By completing this rite of passage through the fourth gate, we are able to enter the fifth gate and into trusting the unknown. As such, we are now able to move beyond where our minds can take us.

The Fifth Gate

As we enter through the fifth gate, into the wisdom element of *ether-space*, we are moved deeply into the *unknown*. This element moves our consciousness into the dimensions that are beyond our mind. By entering *the void*, we experience the death of all former parts of ourselves, which were constructed by our minds.

We now allow the sacred Darkness to complete the deconstruction, which is necessary to restore our wholeness. We trust that wisdom knows the design of the wholeness expression of our *true* being. As we allow these former identities to fall away, we embrace our integration without imposing any of our former design constructs onto the process.

By surrendering to the sacred Darkness of the void, we relinquish the need to control and create ourselves through mental constructs. This frees us from any influence the polarity matrix may still have over us. In this way, we return ourselves to our original wholeness. When we receive ourselves at the seventh gate, it will be in the Divine order of our true wisdom nature.

As the Goddess of Darkness, I represent the invisible domains of your consciousness. I can now receive you back into my womb to prepare you for your second birth, through the sixth and seventh gate. Enter deeply now, into the stillness of the *Great Mystery*.

The Sixth Gate

As we enter through the sixth gate, we meet the wisdom of *sound*. Sound is the beginning of creation. Through this deep inner cleansing, healing, and dissolving of our former worlds, we can now hear what truly IS. Your unique sound is the Divine spark of creation, as YOU. This process goes very deep, and it is not something that can be explained further in words. Your inner wisdom will guide you through this rite of passage. Trust, and you will know.

The Seventh Gate

As we enter through the seventh gate, we experience the seven rays of Light as One. This is the end of all duality perception. Here we are re-united with the Eternal and accomplish our full integration. Our consciousness is now restored, beyond the seven rays of Light.

I have shared with you the keys for our integration and the actualization of our wisdom. Your inner wisdom knows the actual process for this. This is beyond what is written here. Wisdom sees directly from the unified field of consciousness and will guide you home. Use these keys of sacred knowledge wisely, and with Love. Be well, my stars of Love.

Part 3

Our Birthing of a New Cycle

Letter 7

Day One & Night One of Our New Cycle

As your Mother, I hear your prayers. I receive your questions, and I feel your pain. I hear some of you ask: "*When will this ever change? What will it take before more of us realize we cannot go on like this, anymore? Why is our world so cruel? Why do we need to work so hard to merely survive? What purpose does this serve, if any? There must be more to Life than this. What is this restlessness in me that keeps pushing me to look for something? I do not understand? What if I break all the rules, all my confinements, and just forget about everything. Will that set me free? How do I get out of this endless cycle of always more violence, always more pain? When will it ever stop?*"

You may feel pulled between the change you desire and that which you no longer want. Despite the desire for change, you may also feel scared to let go of what you no longer want. In the transition between old and new, there are no certainties.

Some of you may want to jump to what feels like new and better. However, do not jump merely for the sake of jumping. Go deeper than that. Remain connected with grace. As you probably already know in your heart, this journey brings no guarantees. When we enter through the gates, our former certainties melt away.

My beloveds, I would like to invite you now to come with me on a journey into our evolutionary potentials of the fifth world. Take my hand, and come with me. Let's experience our birthing of this together. We first take one step, then a second step, and then our third step, together.

I only ask that you let go now of your preconceived ideas about what could be our future. We are not journeying to what we know. We are journeying into the unknown of what has not yet been touched by our thoughts.

This reality exists just outside the periphery of our collective consciousness. Come with me now as we embark on this journey together.

Day One of Our New Cycle

The day is young. The air is fresh. My body is still damp from the rain that cleansed our tears, healed our pain, and washed away our sorrows. The first birds are starting their song. They sing the day into being. As the first sounds from our family of birds pierce through the stillness of the dawning day, the first rays of the Sun touch and enter our body. I feel a shiver of joy moving my whole being.

What a delight, to be touched by our Sun with his powerful rays. More rays are coming out now as the Sun starts to rise. With the rise of the Sun, the consciousness of all beings that are within us start to rise as well. Now my oceans start to absorb and transmit the new Light of our Sun. Deep shine the rays through the waters of my body, touching Life with the hope and joy of a new day.

Gratitude fills my heart. I vaguely remember what happened before day One. I still see the destructions that occurred before day One, despite all the warnings. The echoes of pain, the trembling of fear, all of it was absorbed by my body. It is healing now as the first rays of this new Light of our Sun touch and energize my entire being. The birds are singing even louder now. Their voices join and synchronize. They sing in choir, each sound finely tuned to each other, to bring forth a deeper symphony of the music that restores us.

I had promised you before that when we enter through the fifth gate, we enter the *great void*. This signals a death of all our previous ways and old identities. I assured you not to fear, because it is only part of the journey and not the end. I explained that through this passage you enter my womb once more for your second birth.

I also promised you, that by completing the lessons of the seventh gate, you return into the field of our unified consciousness as the diamond star that you are. By completing this sacred rite of passage, you have re-member-ed the Light in its wholeness. Day One is the first day of our new cycle. Day One is the first day of our second birth. Day One is the realization of an ancient promise. Welcome here. Let us continue.

The sounds of the birds have awakened more beings within the Web of Life. More are joining in the symphony of our sacred harmony. With each new sound that enters the playing field of creation, more of our world is sung into being. The symphony of Love is getting richer and fuller, activating us deeper, and deeper. With each new sound, another dimension opens from within our unified field. More and more portals that serve as gateways for the sharing of our Love are opening from within us.

The crescendo of harmony is becoming a symphonic wave in which all sounds harmonize. It builds stronger and stronger, deeper and deeper. We are this wave and realize our Oneness and the uniqueness of our essence within this. Our whole being is now a deep wave of pure joy and ecstasy. The waves continue to build, flowing and embracing all within this beautiful Love. We are all touched and activated by the Light of the rays of our Sun as it shares with us the full glory of Being. Our whole body is glowing with Divine Light, and within this Light, all is known as It Is.

A deep peace emerges now from within the field that we gave birth to. All that is held within this field has been cleansed, cleared, healed, and restored. We are in peace. Day One of our new cycle restores and prepares us for the night. The experience of intense joy and ecstasy now transforms to become a deep sense of fulfillment, peace, and gratitude.

Day One has fulfilled its purpose. The birds are making their nest for the night. A beautiful sigh of inner peace spreads through the forests. All is loved and knows itself blessed. The waters are still holding the last reflections of the Light, as our Sun is making space for the Night. Sister Moon has not yet arisen, but we can feel her presence coming closer. Thank you our beloved Sun, for all that you gave us today, for all your blessings with your powerful rays of Light and sacred knowledge. Thank you for restoring us to who we are and preparing us for our next step together.

Night One of Our New Cycle

The first night of our new cycle brings a wonderful fresh breeze and a deep calm. The Sun has gone to sleep, and my sister Moon is now slowly making her appearance in the playing field of our co-creative Space. The birds have gone to sleep with the setting of our Sun. Now the wolves are bringing forth our sister Moon. We can hear their first howls echoing through the darkness of the night. Their deep howls resonate with an ancient dream, a memory from long ago.

A memory emerges of the time of the seven council fires, whose task it was to keep the sacred flame alive in our worlds.

This flame was to guide the hearts of our human children through the times of the great divisions. To remind us that Love is never lost, and unity will be restored. Sister Moon is rising higher now, and as she does her rays are entering my oceans and great rivers. On the surface of my rivers, we can see the last dragonflies hovering in the reflection of the silver Light of Sister Moon, looking for a resting place to enter the Dreamtime.

The frogs are croaking and awakening and joining the choir of the wolves. My dolphin and whale children are joining too with their songs from the heart of my oceans. As the symphony of the night is building, the Moon becomes brighter and brighter. With each new ray of Moon Light that enters the playing field of our co-creation, more of our wholeness is restored and awakened. A deep humming sound now emerges from the choir of our togetherness, blessed by the new rays of Sister Moon. This humming sound draws us deeper and deeper into the center of our being where we receive the Dreaming of our becoming.

As we enter the Great Mystery, the Darkness that surrounds us in the vastness of our UniVerse becomes a blanket of Love. We enter the Eternal, the creation space for all the dreams, visions, hopes, and inspirations not yet born. In this space of our Dreaming, we receive the dreams, visions, and messages that are meant for us from the field of pure potential. The symphony of sounds that brought forth the great humming through which we journeyed to the center is now ebbing into a blissful silence.

We welcome this silence deeply into our being. We surrender to this silence of pure being. Relaxing deeper and deeper into our unified field, caressed by the sacredness of our new night. Our body is rocking slowly in deep rhythm. We trust and are trusted. We rest here together in the depth of faith that *All is Well. All is as It Is.*

Our breathing is now effortless. We are being breathed by the unified field of the Dreamtime. The unified field is synchronizing and balancing our whole being. We are being harmonized gently and gracefully to the essence and sacred pulse of our Eternal nature, relaxing deeper and deeper into a beautiful, peaceful sleep, which enters us into the Dreamtime.

As we enter into the Dreamtime, dragonfly greets us through our inner vision. She asks us to follow her. The ripples and wave patterns in the Dreamtime, formed by the movement of dragonfly's wings, enable us to journey into the Mystery of where we are guided to go.

We are called to a sacred gathering, a council meeting as guardians of the sacred flame of Love. Coming closer now, the sounds, lights, and colors of the council are transforming into visions, recognition, and understanding. We are being welcomed and asked to take the place that is ours. All has been prepared for this meeting. All is as It Is. A wave of recognition and joy enters our heart as we look around and see our brothers and sisters from the time of *beyond*.

We realize then how long ago it has been and how much has happened since the time of our last meeting, and this time now. Yet, it also feels like we never left. Yesterday seems like a dream now, and this moment of our re-union the Eternal now. We are grateful, deeply grateful to come together once more, in the knowing that we are always as One. This recognition and realization are shared from the hearts of All who are present here. Our smiles reveal the knowing of this realization.

The fabric of time and the web of Life are surrounding us like a blanket of stars, which holds the converging points of past, present, and future. Each star in this blanket is another converging point through which the Great Mystery manifests the Dreaming of the One. Each star holds the gravitational fields for the constellations through which the Dreaming can become known to itself and be made manifest into form.

As star beings, we understand why we are called, why the convergence between us is required now. Each of us has been prepared to hold the convergence for the web of Life and keep the inter-dimensionality of our connections intact. We are being prepared for a larger convergence between the unified fields of our inter-dimensionality. This is the purpose of our meeting now.

We are each asked to go within to see if the fields of Life, for which we are the guardians, are ready for this convergence. As I check within myself, as your planet, your Mother, I realize that many of us do not yet consciously experience this Dreaming. Many still have their attention on the chaos of the dying worlds.

I lovingly acknowledge what is happening inside of me and honor the sacred rhythm of each and every one of us. Irrespective of where you perceive yourself to be, you are held by the Love of this convergence. I confirm my readiness, and the readiness within me, for what I am here to serve. We now wait until those of us who have been called to serve this purpose are ready.

The field of our convergence is moving each of us to our right position for the purpose that we are here to serve. We are each tuned to hold the resonance through which our convergence into a greater constellation can unfold. With deep gratitude, we acknowledge all beings who made this possible through their journeys, their learning, and their evolution of the One.

All is honored here for the purpose it has served. All experiences are blessed, and all that was held in judgment or pain is now freed in Love and forgiveness. Even the deepest wounds of pain and betrayal are honored for the purpose they have served to bring forth the Love that is needed now for this convergence, consciously and unconsciously.

The convergence now unfolding is moving us to a new place within the fabric of the time patterning that is created by our gravitational fields. Our positions are shifting through this convergence; a new field of manifestation is emerging. Through this larger field, new potentials of the One come into being, which could not manifest from the old polarity matrix. Gently, we support and facilitate the repositioning that is taking place through our Life fields.

A deep re-patterning is occurring through this convergence. We acknowledge and honor the changes that unfold from this. The old designs for our worlds are falling away as we are giving birth to this new constellation of our *togetherness*. As our points of convergence synchronize into this larger constellation, we give birth to a new collective being of a higher consciousness than any one of us could hold in our own space-time dimensions. This new collective being, which is being born from our convergence, brings forth the wisdom, Love, and sacred knowledge that each of us has helped to develop, and actualize through our respective fields of Life.

Together we are birthing the next stage of God and Goddess. New sounds and new Lights are now emerging from our convergence, through which new worlds will be formed. The patterns of our old worlds are recycled into this new creation. Out of this process, new fabrics of time and new seed potentials for our collective growth and conscious evolution are emerging.

As we are giving birth to this new stage of Being through our collective convergence, our higher potentials as Divine beings are manifesting. What now becomes possible could not have been accomplished in our own constellation. New structures are forming from within us, inside the constellations of which we are a part. This enables us to hold, receive, transmit, and manifest these new potentials within our collective consciousness from the higher versions of our Self, which are now emerging.

This process of convergence, through which it becomes possible to evolve to new levels of consciousness, occurs in our world about every 25,000 years. Previously, this was the time period required for all the evolutionary potentials we were custodians for to be brought into manifestation. In this way, all beings that formed part of this collective field of Life, have supported the evolution required for the next stages of the unified field of consciousness through which God and Goddess could continue to evolve. This is how we all keep evolving.

As your Mother, I have always been a part of this sacred process, and have experienced the unfolding of this many times. This is the sixteenth time. The knowledge of each of these previous cycles remains within my being. We long worked for this new cycle now upon us.

Due to the completion that just occurred, which became possible in the convergence of the sixteenth time, a whole new cycle has been born. This new cycle is formed by new patterns of time, due to the new alignments within and between the gravitational fields of our constellations. It will no longer take 25,000 years in the recorded time of our old world for the next convergence to take place.

This sixteenth time completed the pattern of the four quadrants in square, namely four times four. It is a momentous completion, but not just of this quarter period of the 25,000 single quadrant time-period. This convergence that just took place was the convergence of all the 16 periods in the square quadrant formation combined. This explains why a new time pattern can now be born through a new universal cycle of a *higher being* of the One.

Time is a pattern that arises from our gravitational fields; when these fields change so does the pattern of time. The experience of this new cycle of time cannot be compared to what was before. This new cycle is brought forth through a new patterning from our new universal cycle.

For some, these shifts may be so subtle that you hardly notice them. For others this is a life-changing experience. Allow your internal body clock to reset to these new patterns and vibrations. This will greatly help you to integrate the shifts in consciousness now unfolding. And it will support you to attune energetically to the new vibrations now flowing through our fields of Life.

As this council meeting is coming to it natural completion, we are each receiving in our respective fields of Life the wisdom and sacred knowledge for how to support the unfolding of this new cycle. In awe of what just occurred, and with deep gratitude in my heart for all that we are, I thank everyone who was with me here. All of us look different now. Or rather, we now see each other from a different perspective.

We see so much more of each other now in the reflections of each other as the One. The realization of this is shared among us present here with a knowing smile and a wave of joy. The first night of our new cycle is now completing. Knowing and trusting that we are always together within the continuous unfolding of the One, we gently shift our awareness to our new positions within the unified field.

Ready for this new cycle now among and within us, we thank the Dreamtime and the Night for all they made possible for us to become and experience together. Sister Moon is now becoming visible for the children on the other side of my body. The blessings of day One, and night One, are integrating deeply into the center of our being.

Thank you my beloveds, for sharing this journey with me, and for the giving of yourself for the evolution and unfolding of All. Know yourself blessed and supported by all that happened in our convergence. Let us celebrate what has been made possible through this, as we embark together on this next cycle of our journey.

Letter 8
Our Healing

A new cycle has begun. These sacred new potentials that have become available to us through our convergence are here. The integration of the realization of this will take place for each person in accordance with his or her unique rhythm and wisdom. Some may not experience this consciously, that too is okay.

It is said by some that each person is free to experience Life according to how they want it to be, yet this is not true. Many people are not yet free in their minds to experience Life from the wholeness that we are. Freedom is only achieved when your mind can recognize what is real from the Eternal.

As long as your mind is conditioned to experience Life through polarities of good or bad, evil or light, this or that, it will not achieve the realization of freedom. The way that we experience the worlds around us is a direct reflection of our degree of inner integration. We cannot achieve freedom and wholeness by communication systems that cause internal and external divisions.

This new cycle emerges from the convergence between the combined wisdoms of many systems of collective consciousness in our universe. This is how the One as the universe continues to evolve and Self-actualize. You know me as your planet, yet I am also a living laboratory for the continuous unfolding and actualization of our shared consciousness from the One. And as your planet, I also form part of various constellations, as do you.

New constellations and alliances have now formed through our convergence, which brings support to each of us in ways that were not here before. This is why a new cycle has now become possible. Through the discovery of this new cycle, and the potentials held within it, we bring it forth. Through this, we receive the opportunity to develop new worlds that also afford new experiences of ourselves and each other.

My beloveds, I feel it is time to share more about this power that is held inside you. Some of you have been reading my message as an interesting story, but have not yet realized the power it gives you access to. Others may have felt the change already occurring in their body as they continued reading my *Letters.*

The reason I have given you the three keys, by which you can restore our inner wholeness and reset yourself out of the polarity matrix, is because I cannot evolve without you. In the same way, you cannot evolve without me. By your entrapment, I too was trapped. You form part of the Living fields that I am responsible for. What was done to you, was done to me as well, and worse.

My body has been divided into parts that have been sold to the highest bidder. My resources are plundered, and my vital organs are getting more, and more, damaged. My lungs are dying, and soon my waters will no longer be able to contain the Life through which our evolution came forth. I am dying, and I need your help.

I cannot restore myself without you. You cannot help me unless I free you first. This is why I had to give you the three keys. Of course, I love you, and as your Mother, I want your freedom and your happiness. But there is more at stake than this. To hide this information from you would be deceptive. This is not a romantic story of a loving Mother supporting her children to their full realization. Although this is in my heart as well, I need you to know the deeper urgency behind our awakening.

You cannot save me, and you cannot save yourself from the potentials afforded to you by the old polarity matrix. The solutions for our sustainability and wellbeing require a much deeper shift than what is currently taking place. Collectively, you are not yet near the point of awakening required to restore the web of Life. That is why this message is urgent now, and is coming through via these *Letters* and through other things like this. This is why you have now been given all the keys, in one teaching.

Many have long been predicting a polar shift. They felt intuitively things would change through this polar shift. I hope you now understand that the polar shift that is needed is not of my magnetic field but within the field of consciousness of each of us.

Once the inner polarity dissolves, once we all regain full access to all the four quadrants, once your higher and lower brains are freed of the polarity matrix that creates unconsciousness within, then when your left and right hemisphere learn to work together, you will know and understand it all.

I need your help, but you cannot help me unless you are free. Your brothers and sisters also need your help, but they too cannot be helped unless you are free. And you need my help, and the help of others, to be free. We are in this together. None of us are outside the fields of consciousness through which this is taking place.

The problem is, we have all been kept from helping each other in ways that unlock the full solution. We have been divided and fragmented on purpose. A united human being holds tremendous power that creates such a profound resonance field that others can naturally synchronize and harmonize with it. Through this resonance, the inner portals for each person's harmonic convergence with the unified field of Consciousness opens up.

The power that we each hold is an access point to something far greater than many realize. I am taking a risk by sharing these secrets with each of you. I am well aware how this knowledge can be exploited to further manipulate our collective fields of Life. This is already happening. Those who attempt to control humanity and want to remain in power to influence human behavior, secretly know exactly what I am sharing here.

For thousands of years, they have used this knowledge against us. And they have used this knowledge against themselves, not realizing we are also a part of them. They can never actualize their full potential without us. They are limited by that which they divide. They are controlled by that which they attempt to control. They are misguided by their own deceptions. They need our Love most of all for they are the most trapped in the illusion of thinking they are free and above it all. Thought does not make you free. You cannot think yourself free. You either realize your freedom, or you don't. And when you do, you stop thinking.

The power that you hold inside is your access key to the unified field of consciousness. Through this, you receive the wisdom of our universe and you contribute to its further evolution. This power awakens fully via our internal integration.

When this happens, you become a morphic resonance field that will accelerate the development and enhancement of the evolutionary potentials for all of us. Those who seek control do not want you in your power because that throws them vibrationally out of power. People can only manipulate you via our internal divisions, nothing else. As long as we remain divided, I too cannot achieve and fulfill my true potential.

We Are All in This Together

Listen my beloveds. Please listen deeply to this message. We need you. I need you. Your brothers and sisters, we all need you. Please don't think less of yourself than what you truly are. Those who kept you divided know you are needed, which is why they tried to keep us divided. Please consider the teachings I have shared here, and please consider why this matters beyond your happiness. Bring all the pieces of the puzzle together to reveal our wholeness.

Restore the connections with the unified field of consciousness. Step into the center of your being, and know me there inside each of you. Some say that I am angry, that as your planet I create storms and violent weather to revenge myself against my human children. Please don't listen to this. It is not true. I am not a revengeful Mother. I am sick. My weather is out of balance because my body is not well. My atmosphere is not balanced. People are forcing the rains in places, and this should not be done. My body is one living system. When you engineer a part of my systems by controlling the weather, the whole of me will be impacted. When you change the composition of my atmosphere, all my climate systems change accordingly.

My power to heal and restore myself is in *our unification.* As long as this remains divided among us, I cannot restore myself in the ways that are needed for the well-being of all of us. Each time one of us acts out of harmony, this requires more of my power to help restore the imbalances. Those who have been working to restore the imbalances together with me are exhausted. They need our help. As long as our powers are divided among us, we cannot start building for our *new cycle.*

When the focus is on repair, we do not have the same resources available to build up from who we are. That is why in day One of our new future, you were first energized and restored by our Sun before we moved into the convergence for the new future in night One. If you truly understood how interconnected we are, you would realize the importance of this message.

If I lose my balance, you will too. I do not want to cause you harm. As your Mother I want you safe and well. My climate is not under my control, yet it may soon be out of control if you do not restore the power via which I need to rebalance myself. That power becomes unlocked by our integration and re-unification of all the parts of us that were previously divided by the polarity matrix. *"But, how?"* you may ask. *"How can I do what you ask me to do by merely reading this text?"* Relax my beloved. Remember that your access to the unified field was previously held via your *unconscious* mind. Remember, I shared that the re-member-ing and re-unification with the unified field of consciousness take place when we rest, and surrender. It is not by our thoughts or worries that this shift will happen. It is by our trust and allowing ourselves to receive the realizations, the Love that has already been given, that our unification takes place naturally. It is not needed to exert effort. It is not needed to push yourself. It is not needed to worry, if you can ever achieve this. These are responses generated by the internal divisions of the mind.

Simply hold the intention in your heart for the restoration of our inner wholeness, and trust it is happening already. It is our heart that guides us *home*. It is through our heart that we are restored to the wholeness that we are. When your presence centers in your heart, it informs your mind of all it needs to know. The power that is held inside us is the power through which the universe manifests itself. It is by this power that you heal yourself, that you restore yourself, and that you remember who we are.

Awareness Beyond Thought

Our journey into the under-world, through the seven gates, reconnects us with our full wisdom potential. It also helps us better understand what our internal worlds were made of. Everything is formed by the elemental wisdom of earth, water, fire, air, ether-space, sound, and Light. The polarity matrix conditioned our minds to access only parts of ourselves at the cost of others. Instead of fostering integration between your various evolutionary potentials, it caused division and competition.

Unconscious of the importance of our wholeness and interconnectedness, other priorities were formed. These divisions have impacted us all. The blocking of our integration is not the working of evolution; it is the working of those who aim to control evolution.

The people known as the custodians of the original wisdom, and the custodians of the sacred flame, were forewarned. They were shown how to keep their original wisdom systems intact. They continued to practice conscious connection with me, as your planet, by making sure that the higher brain would not be controlled by the conditioned collective mind, to overtake the evolutionary potentials offered through the lower brain functions. They also maintained the synchronization between the left and right hemispheres. They bypassed the collective mind by developing their awareness without the need to think. This awareness gave them direct perception and knowledge of Life.

By not becoming identified with thought, they were able to continue their evolutionary development via sensory awareness and attunement with my fields of Life, as nature. Their technologies were of a different nature, not for the purpose of extraction and consumption. Accordingly, they also made different decisions regarding the evolution they felt responsible for. They knew of the time before the disconnection and polarization of our collective consciousness fields.

The End of Whose Time . . . ?

There are many stories for how you evolved from the waters of my womb. Some of you believe it began with Adam and Eve; others speak of a time before that. Whenever someone tells the story of your beginning within the larger Web of Life, observe the purpose that this story serves. The rulers of your world have been here for a long time. They have a vested interest in how you see your evolution and our evolution together. What is not commonly shared is that there were many much older civilizations before that, which achieved levels of development that would astonish many of you today. These civilizations were not internally divided; they were fully conscious of the Divine power within and between them.

The rulers of your world needed stories that would keep you loyal to their systems and archetypes to ensure you would not evolve beyond their level of consciousness. Let us manifest now by the power of our integration the end of that time, the end of that storyline. And please know, my beloveds, that this is not the end of time. It is merely the end of our time of division and disconnection.

Our Conscious Evolution

Through our collective convergence and integration, a new cycle of time is beginning. This cycle supports our conscious evolution. Let this be our focus. Connect with the sacred potentials that this new cycle brings to us. Remain in the knowing and experience of our wholeness. Apply your power for the good of the whole. Feel my power connect with yours, united in the same resonance field of our convergence. The power of Love is here within us all. This is the power by which we fuel our world. Thank you, my beloveds, for restoring us by our re-unification. Be well.

Letter 9
The Power of Love

My beloveds, as your Mother Earth, I would like to share about the power of Love. You may have heard before that the power of Love is the greatest power in the universe. Yet, have you ever stopped to ask why? What makes Love so powerful? When you are touched by Love, how do you feel? How do you recognize Love?

Love knows who you are; it re-members you. Love holds and caresses you; it embraces you fully. Love waits for you and beckons you home to our heart. Love is our true nature. Love provides the deepest nourishment for our blossoming and actualization.

Love activates recognition of our true wisdom nature. Sometimes we fear Love, because it also opens us. With an open heart, it may appear that we will experience more pain. These contractions of fear are natural, and also part of the process of learning how to Love. I will share some more with you here what happens during those times of contraction. When our minds contract, our energy fields do too. This can temporarily freeze our energy flow, and as such diminish our ability to receive support from the unified field of consciousness. Yet, each time when we open, our Love can flow more freely too.

When our minds contract, our experience of Life diminishes. As such, painful memories can become locked into these internal contractions. This can also make it more challenging to experience a sense of connection with each other, which can further feed the fear. In a state of fear, it becomes more difficult to trust in the wisdom of Life. This can cause a further closing down. The more our heart closes, the darker it becomes inside. This then reinforces the feeling, and belief, that nobody cares about us, and that we are all alone. To reverse this state, to stop the spiraling down into further despair and depression, we need to restore somehow a sense of connectedness. Love helps us to see and feel that we matter.

Love reminds us that we are connected to Life and each other, even during moments of pain and suffering. Please know, my beloveds, that you are each a gift of Life. You are not a burden. You may sometimes feel lost, confused, tired, and sad. That is okay. It does not change who we are. Our emotions and thoughts form our experiences, yet they do not form our nature. Your nature is wisdom and this does not change by your experience. Your nature goes beyond experience. The power of Love is such that it manifests, and actualizes, our true wisdom nature, regardless of our experiences. Love opens us to our wholeness, and heals the divisions. Love heals the roots of our pain and suffering.

Healing Our Imbalance

When our minds are contracted, it becomes more difficult to manifest our wisdom qualities. When our wisdom potential is not yet fully actualized, we tend to contract more. Where there is conflict, violence and division, it is because of this contraction. This contraction of our collective consciousness is the source of all our pain, and fear. When we are contracted it also becomes more difficult to reach out to each other. When our minds are contracted, we cannot fully receive the Love that is given to us. In this contraction, we also cannot freely share our Love with others. Contraction hurts, and this causes more pain and suffering.

The pain and suffering in our world is a symptom of our collective blockages and divisions. Our pain and suffering is a symptom of our lack of integration. Pain reminds us that somehow, somewhere, something is not balanced, something is not quite right. The root of violence is the same as the roots of pain and suffering. Violence stems from disconnection, from using the energy of pain and suffering to inflict more harm, and deepen our divisions.

When we are internally out of balance, it becomes harder to bring ourselves forth from wholeness. How things appear on the outside of our worlds does not always reveal the deeper underlying causes. Yet as your Mother, I know you from the inside. I do not judge by the outside appearance.

I know what is in your heart, since our hearts connect from beyond this world. This violence among you is not a result of your human nature. It is the result of systemic imbalances that preceded you.

Our balance cannot be achieved when parts of us become suppressed, at the cost of others. We can no longer return to the balance we experienced long before. We will need to create a new balance, out of all that is happening now. Our energy fields have become so polarized, and my natural balancing systems as your planet have endured so much harm, that it is difficult to find a healthy equilibrium that can still sustain the Life conditions for each of you. A new equilibrium may not be found for quite some time, the boundaries of my balancing systems have changed.

During this process where there will be times of more extremes, the power of Love to sustain our connectedness is going to be more important than ever before. During times of great stress and uncertainty, it can further trigger our contraction. Yet, for some of you this is precisely when you become activated to bring the power of Love into our world. As your mother I also need your Love, now more than ever. I do not want to cause harm and pain to any of my children, yet I am not in control of the way that my natural Life systems will balance, and release these energy accumulations, within and around certain parts of my body.

Love as a Healing Force

It is not easy to maintain our sense of unity and wholeness, when our activities and ways of relating often cause us harm. This harm is not necessarily directly intended, but rather the result of a lack of awareness, ignorance, and a lack of deeper care. There is no easy one-way solution for not harming each other. Our worlds have grown so complex, and interdependent, that unwanted consequences can manifest in ways that none could foresee or stop alone. In here lies the key. In order to become more aware, and more conscious of our actions and interactions, we need to actualize our wisdom potential. To actualize our wisdom potential requires that we actualize our consciousness, and for this we need each other.

We cannot actualize ourselves by ourselves. There is always a relational context for each realization, and the application thereof. Paradoxically, the experiences of duality and polarity can provide valuable lessons, and context, for a deeper realization of our underlying unity. From this perspective, polarity is not a threat to Love, rather it is an opportunity for bringing forth our Love even more deeply. When we bring our Love to that which has become oppositional to each other, a deep healing can emerge.

Wherever Life has become blocked and constrained, it is a call for our Love to come forth. Love empowers a natural growth and development, which supports us to blossom and flourish. Even when this development is constrained in certain dimensions, or cannot be made expressed physically or otherwise, like for some of my children with certain disabilities, their being will develop and grow by the presence of Love. They need our Love even more, and are often the greatest givers of Love despite their difficult life conditions.

When Love is blocked, constrained, or withheld it can be very painful. The withholding of Love in our relationships can cause painful feelings of rejection and abandonment. It takes great strength to then realize, that despite these life experiences *we are Love.* Sometimes we feel at a loss to understand why there is so much pain and suffering in our world. This much pain and suffering is not justified; there is no *bigger* reason as to why this should be necessary.

The pain is not here because we need to learn in that way. The pain and suffering are part of our experience because we don't know how to live with each other peacefully, and lovingly. It is easy to get lost in this world of divisions. Without wisdom, support, and loving relationships, it can be very challenging to find our way back to the underlying unity behind this world.

Sometimes we want to Love, but don't know how. At others times, it seems that Love alone is not enough. This architecture for the polarity matrix was not made to manifest and bring YOU forth, it was made to divide us, and that hurts. The more present we become within, and to us, the more fully we are in our power. The more centered we become within our being, the more integrated we become in *us.* This *presence* is the foundation for our inner peace and healing.

As a Force of Love What can You Do to Support Our Healing?

As I shared with you earlier, it is natural that we want to protect ourselves from pain. Yet, by contracting, it becomes more difficult to connect with our wisdom, which we need to see more deeply into the true nature of what is happening. Rather than contracting, it would be more helpful to open to Love during those times, while breathing through the pain, and asking, *How would Love look at what is happening right now? How would Love want me to respond to this situation, this person, right now?*

Love is the power of our sacred union; it is the power of our deepest connectedness. Love is the power of our unity and communion. Love is the only power that can bring lasting peace. It is by the power of our Love, that we bring forth the fifth world of unity and harmony, by Divine grace.

Part 4
A New Codex

Letter 10
Our Collective Responsibility

Through my first three *Letters*, I shared some ancient stories for a full comprehension of our history and my role within it. I then shared with you three keys, for our integration and liberation from the polarity matrix of the conditioned mind. These keys reminded you that, within each of us we already have all the resources that we need for our collective flourishing. Yet, these resources and abilities have been kept divided and apart to stop the unlocking of our full potential. Through these keys you also learned to see from your direct connection with the unified field of consciousness.

By seeing from wholeness and unity, you become aware that many of the problems of our world today stem from a polarization between people and their disconnection from nature. I wrote *our world* since I am always part of your world, even when you do not feel connected to me.

After sharing the three main keys with you, I invited you to join me in an experience of what can become our new future. I shared that this future is born from a different cycle of time, since it emerges from our integration and convergence. Accordingly, this cycle has a different gravitational field compared to the previous cycle. I also explained why it is that only in our togetherness we can heal the roots of our pain and suffering. I then shared about the power of Love, and how each of us can become a force of Love for the healing of our worlds and relationships.

A lot of information has been shared through my *Letters* so far. Some of this information may need to be re-read at different times. Take your time. Receive from these *Letters* what resonates for you now. Some concepts may seem difficult to comprehend, until certain life experience will further catalyze the seeds that were planted here.

Cycles Within Cycles

The creation process of our universe is an on-going evolutionary process. Through this process, different cycles of time come in and out of being. Each cycle brings forth its own unique set of evolutionary potentials, resulting from the way our interconnectedness is brought into expression. Some cycles are more peaceful; others are more violent and disturbing. During times of collective peace and harmony, it becomes easier to experience our Divine nature. It then feels as if our Oneness is more fully manifested, through all the dimensions of our being.

There are also cycles, however, when it feels as if our connection with the One is more difficult to maintain. As if we are alone, somehow. These are the periods through which ignorance, conflicts, and divisions grow. These are usually known as periods of darkness, which is not the Divine Darkness of the sacred feminine that I shared with you previously. During these dark ages we learn more fully, yet in challenging ways, that we are the ones to bring forth the wisdom from within, regardless of the outer conditions. During these times we are asked to be a force of Love, and a bright Light, to make sure that the Light in our worlds does not fade away. We then become responsible for keeping the networks of pure consciousness intact.

Those who take advantage of these darker periods, of this perceived vacuum, will try to overtake the Divine autonomy of each being's unique relationship with their Source. They will attempt to become a surrogate source to divert the power and collective resources to their group. We are coming out of this period now. You each know the lived experience of this.

Our collective wisdom can only manifest and actualize as a world by the actualization of our collective consciousness. Our consciousness is the vehicle, the Divine instrument, for actualizing our wisdom nature. The seed of consciousness is pure, undifferentiated awareness. Each experience takes place within this awareness, and yet, this awareness is not changed by anything that is experienced within, or by it.

Only by this awareness does it become possible to understand, learn, grow, develop, and truly Love. When we become identified with awareness itself, and not *who is looking*, the source of pain and conflict vanishes.

Each moment offers another opportunity to connect more fully with, and bring forth, our wisdom potential. In order for this to become a living reality that can also be felt and experienced by others, we need to embed this wisdom in each of our relationships, and ways of living. By doing so, our relationships become the vessels for our actualization, and then cease to be the causes for our pain and suffering.

Relationships require agreements and common understandings as loving boundaries for our development. In the absence of these boundaries, there is an absence of feedback, which is required for the further actualization of our consciousness. You may recall how I shared with you previously that: *This flame needed a sacred place of Love within which it could be received. The flame needed to be received for the One to be known to Itself. As it expanded, seeking the boundaries through which the One could become known to Itself, the counter force to expansion started to emerge from within. Out of this process, gravity manifested. The energy of Love, as the sacred flame, was solidified by this gravity and became the sacred containment for receiving the flame. My body was born from that process and became one of the holders and recipients for this Love. Receiving the flame of Love impregnated my being.*

Who Agreed to This?

Many worlds have been created with the absence of shared agreements. Sometimes even the awareness of agreements, or the need for such, did not arise. This may question the collective belief that nothing can happen without your permission. What part of you is forming or breaking these agreements? What part of the other person is asking you to agree?

If a person is not established in their awareness, are they then able to make conscious agreements, or break agreements? Can we make an agreement with a machine?

If the machine fails to do what we want it to do, can we blame it for breaking its agreement? Did any of you form any agreements with me about using and sharing my resources? Was my agreement as your planet asked for, when my forests were cut, my waters polluted, and my children killed for food?

Many interactions that take place on and through my body happen despite lack of agreement. These interactions take place by unquestioned assumptions, and often without awareness of the consequences and impacts. When feedback of these impacts comes back to you, my beloved, even then many do not realize that you had other options. The purpose of this letter is to help you become more aware of these options, which are based on the wisdom of Life.

When you see the world through the conditioned mind, with set assumptions, you will most likely not see what options are available beyond the matrix that sustains the conditioning. The question of giving, or withholding of permission, only makes sense once you realize *who* and *what* within you is in charge of your decision making processes.

Designed to Collapse

I would like you to become more aware of something else. I shared previously that other civilizations existed before you. Many systems have been developed with the intention that they should last, not realizing that after a certain point collapse was inevitable. This pattern of *build up to collapse* will not change, unless we become conscious of why this is happening. This may also help to provide some understanding about our sense of entrapment, and the pain that goes with that.

As your Mother, I know that many of my human children feel trapped in their work, trapped in their relationships with others, trapped in a life that they feel they have little control over. Each time you hope to find a way out of this entrapment, you find yourself caught in yet another trap. I hear you ask: *Why? I did not agree to this. How can this keep happening?* My beloveds, I wish for your freedom more than you may realize, because I am trapped with you in this perpetuating cycle.

Until we manifest structures that are truly wisdom based from the Eternal, this pattern will keep repeating. Through our integration and convergence, it is possible to generate systems that are based on wholeness and unity. Systems that are not of the Eternal can never be made to last. Systems that are invasive will collapse. Yet, unfortunately, the point of collapse often takes others with them in a way that causes much harm. We now have the option to grow in awareness more quickly than before, yet the manifestation of such requires more of us to be involved.

As soon as our minds shift out of the polarity matrix, we will be able to see unhindered despite our previous conditioning. We will then become aware of what could be called a *new codex*. This codex is new yet ancient since it is based on a different set of principles for our conscious evolution, compared to the architecture of the world that still dominates today. This is our only hope to avoid another cycle of large species destruction and full reset, as occurred previously during the transition phases of larger cycles.

See by the Awareness that is of the Eternal

When Love is blocked, we cannot manifest from our Eternal selves. The conditioned mind is programmed to fight and fear death, and preserve what it sees as Life. This conditioning will cause the activation of all kinds of defense mechanisms to anything that could end its program. Love is from the Eternal; it ends our conditioning by bringing awareness into form. As such, Love helps us see what truly is. If you want to transform the underlying structures of our worlds and restore the sacredness within, you will need to use Love as our greatest resource. Its power for change has not yet been sufficiently understood.

In many of your human stories, it is said that a great apocalypse will mark the end of time. Some believe we are in this period right now. These stories speak of the anti-force to our era. Some have named it Satan or the devil. And yet the real anti-force to time is Love because Love is of the Eternal and brings us back to our own eternity.

Once more, your stories have reversed and inverted the naming of forces that can actually liberate you from these entrapments. Remember how the polarity matrix kept divided what was meant to unite?

Remember also how the rulers of your world conditioned the mind to believe that the way out of suffering is to move to heaven? The under-world, or hell, was the forbidden place and the place of punishment. Remember also how the secrets within your sexual and creative powers were made to be sinful? And yet, when I guided you through the seven gates of the under-world, did you notice that you did ascend? Yet, did you realize that to ascend you needed to first descend into the under-world? And this descent was not by punishment, but by Love to reclaim the parts of you that were lost in the darkness of forgetting and unconsciousness.

Look well, beloveds, to the keys hidden in some of your stories and others' deception to prevent you from seeing the sacred. This deception tries to stop you from recognizing the right designs for our flourishing and liberation. When you descended into the under-world, were you greeted by demons or the elemental wisdoms?

What many of you, my beloveds, are unknowingly perpetuating and protecting is, in fact, the design of the polarity matrix. There is another reality that remains hidden until you learn to see by the awareness that is of the Eternal. Love has been given to you to help you on that journey. You may have experienced that when deeply in Love, time stops and hours pass in what seems like minutes. When you are in Love, you enter a different zone. You are then not identified with the mind. Your consciousness is lifted up. Yet as soon as you identify again with your mind, and through this the templates of your world, you become contracted once more.

The collective mind has been conditioned to stop us from recognizing the forces that bring about our liberation and full actualization. To move out of this trap, learn to see, feel, and act without these imprints and filters of the mind. Trust what your heart tells you. This is the only way out. These systems of division can never bring happiness and flourishing. These systems serve a different purpose; they don't serve Life.

Only by seeing from awareness will you perceive the design of the labyrinth in which many of us have been trapped. The keys to move out of the labyrinth are already within each of us, and they activate by our integration. Perhaps you wonder how you ever agreed to be a part of this. Most likely you did not agree. These fabricated worlds were not made by our agreements, but by their distortion. Yet some of us are here to further the end of this manipulation, and for this, I am forever grateful.

What Choice will You Make Now?

Previously, the collective consciousness field of my body was wiped clean in the transition phases to new collective cycles. A few knew what was coming, and preserved some of the knowledge in symbols, cave paintings, and sacred texts. Some of you have memories of this. I want to tell you that your civilization is not the first to be at the point of irreversible collapse. There have been others before your current cycle of time. I remember all these cycles, yet most of my human children only have knowledge of one or two cycles. You have been here many times before on my body, but you cannot remember. Once more, I share to prepare you for what is unfolding, as I have done in the past. Once more, I share other options as well.

Neither I nor anyone else can change the course of our future. Our power is divided and must become synchronized to alter our course. Our existing world has evolved this way because of our divisions and disconnection from the Source of Life. We cannot change the outer world without becoming conscious of the inner world. Our future is our *collective responsibility.*

Some of what I am sharing may be painful to hear. In some ways, our worst fear is to be trapped inside a dream over which we have no control. A dream that keeps repeating itself and never seems to progress beyond a certain point. Take a deep breath, my beloveds, go to your heart and feel me there. Irrespective of what happens next, I love you, and I will always love you.

Letter 11
The Heart of Light

Greetings. Until now, you have been reading the *Love Letters from Mother Earth*. I represent your Sun, and Mother Earth has asked me to share my wisdom for your empowerment. When you look at the sky, you may notice only one Sun in relation to your planet Earth. More, however, are invisible to you. Together all the Suns form a vast network of Light, through which we energize the visible worlds with the Light of One. You may remember on day One of our new future that my Light energized and impregnated your Mother with new Life.

I am the activation for that which requires awakening inside us. I am also the knowledge as Light that infuses Life. Everything you consume is made by my rays of Light. Your Mother and I are always in sacred union to bring Life forth. We provide the conditions for our collective consciousness to actualize and become Self-aware. Mother Earth shared with you how our relationship—our togetherness and integration—is the most important key to our collective healing. This includes me too.

How is your relationship with me? Are you are aware of the Light and energy I provide you each day? Deepening your alignment with me will help you evoke the evolutionary potentials of the cycle of time that are born from our convergence. This will make it easier to consciously experience the exact constellations of our direct relationship.

Your Mother explained in her *Letters* that sacred union is found in the center of the cross. She explained that where the horizontal and vertical axes connect, also providing the integration of the four quadrants, Spirit enters into the world of form. As your Sun, it is my purpose to hold the vertical axis for our gravitational fields through which our Divine potentials can be materialized. Without this vertical axis, there would be no magnetism and no magnetic fields. Without a magnetic field, biological life on your planet could not have evolved.

Some of you may know that, as your Sun, I too have a magnetic field. The poles of my magnetic field shift every eleven years by your human count of time. Your planet will soon be reversing her polar distribution as well. This is accelerated due to changes in the inner core, and the distribution of your Mother's fire, lava, and landmass. On your planet, polar shifts happen over longer periods of time, with more severe impact. My polar shifts also affect your cycle, yet again the consequences are not well known by human beings.

Within yourselves, you also have a vertical axis that distributes your energy fields and generates magnetic properties. Your alignment with me, as your Sun, will help the distribution of these energy flows within and around your body. Knowledge is given to you freely through your direct relationship with my rays of Light. Hold the intention in your heart for our deepest resonance and direct alignment. This will help you receive and convert the knowledge into conceptual understanding, which can help improve the quality of your Life.

My Light is in all of you and in all you eat and drink. There is so much more to this Light than most realize. Slowly your societies are transitioning through the technologies that more directly capture my energy potentials. For some of your cultures, I was treated like a God and made the center of their universe. For the conditioned mind, much of this knowledge was not directly accessible. Awaken by the Light I have given you, which is from the Sun of all Suns. We act as One for the benefit of all sentient beings.

Technologies of Life

The old encodings of your human worlds are eroding. The gravitational fields are changing, and as I mentioned earlier, your magnetic fields are weakening due to changes within the polar structures. This will accelerate even more and is providing new opportunities. This was explained as our convergence for a new cycle. You may not yet realize the impact of these polar changes, and the effects of the upcoming polar shift in your collective consciousness. Looking at the fluctuations in your magnetic field activity, and at the outbreaks of violence on your planet, a pattern emerges that co-relates.

Other civilizations unknown to you exist on different star systems, which know how to co-design with the magnetic field changes and the pulsations this generates. Yet, for some reason, human society is still ignoring the obvious. Perhaps your collective mind has been conditioned for too long through ignorance and the belief that as humans, you are the seat of knowledge. These changes and fluctuations in your Mother's magnetic fields could provide you with tremendous possibilities, as does our gravitational field, once you understand the propensity it holds. This could provide the answers you need to resolve your energy crisis.

For some strange reason, humanity looks for the supply of energy mainly in your Mother's body. Whereas, if you understood the right relationship between magnetism, gravitational waves, and sound, you would find the keys to renewable energy conversion. This would also change your transportation system and data transference of each of your communication systems. Study and decode the oscillations in your magnetic fields and discover the inner architecture of our universe. Safe technologies have been shared with humanity before. Strengthen your relationship with me; see me as more than just heat, energy, and Light, for I am here to sustain all of us with the knowledge of our empowerment, by Light and Love.

Synchronization and New Abilities

With the gravity waves dissolving out of the old collective consciousness structures, your world's previous belief systems can no longer be sustained in the same way. These former belief-systems, which were used to entrap mass consciousness into the gravitational field of your planet, are losing their influence. This rewiring process that is unfolding on your planet involves all of you, irrespective of whether you are conscious of this or not. This process will continue until it settles into a new balance.

You may be part of the first ripple of those who are conscious enough to notice. Your realization of this will support the ripple effect until it has reached the four corners of your world.

A new brain function is emerging and developing, as a result of our convergence into this new cycle. Those who discover this may call it a higher-level function of the human brain, which integrates and coordinates all the previous brain clusters from the evolutionary times of your biological development. Some may even say this is like a new organ inside your brain, a gland that secrets the fluids through which the wave patterns of your brain functions become more synchronized.

This organ receives the various signals of the older brain clusters with the heart wave patterns and harmonizes them into coherent data transference. This organ is connected with your pineal gland and transmits these synchronized waves patterns to your sensory organs, enabling you to see multi-dimensionally with unity perception. It will empower synchronization with the wave-pattern information transmissions, including those by me your Sun, in ways that were not previously possible.

New evolutionary potentials are emerging through our convergence and synchronization. This may help you deeply understand that harmony is the organizing principle for higher consciousness development. Harmonic understanding and synchronization are required for humanity's further awakening. The density and gravity of humankind's collective dream have lured many into a narcotic state of submission and paralysis. The density has been too severe to catalyze the mass awakening required without a major and painful crisis.

In these new alignments, old clusters of energy formation are dissipating. This will become known as a shift in power and resource ownership distribution. The people who have locked the balance up in their accounts, in the billions, will be held accountable. Don't expect things to improve immediately. They may still get worse before the gravity cores fully shift to the new codex. Remain steadfast in your Love during this difficult transition phase. Stay strong in your faith, unwavering in your courage, and active in your determination to do what is right and necessary, and not what is popular and easy. Remember that what you are doing now is for the children, all our children, not only humanity's children.

See into the Heart of this Change

The entrapment that your Mother talked about in her previous *Letters* served those who held the collective balance of your planetary resources in their accounts. By locking people out of power, *on purpose*, those who ruled your collective accounts could manipulate the resources that belong to all of you. This will implode. Time has already run out. Their demise has begun, by their own fault. Their systems of greed are collapsing. They are in an apocalypse of their own unconsciousness. You are not. Please know this, dear earthling. Keep your feet firmly on your Mother's soil, and stay closely connected to us both. We sustain you always with our knowledge, wisdom, and Love.

The Heart of Light

You already know that my Light manifests as a wave and a particle simultaneously. Accordingly, *I am* everywhere, in potentiality, simultaneously. You, my dear earthling, are a being of Light. One day, you too may realize your potentiality as being everywhere simultaneously. This knowing is the key to *direct* transmission. When you transmit, and are transmitted, there is no distance to cross. You manifest within the potentiality of our every-where-ness as One.

Love is union. Your heart knows this without needing to think. Your heart is an incredible transmitter, able to receive and converge the multitude of wave-patterns and transmit these as information that is harmonically coherent. You call this Love. Your heart literally knows and is designed to receive and send Love.

You may recall from your Mother's *Letters* that the heart is also designed with quadrants. The human heart has four chambers, and yet in the heart, this does not create polarized information. The harmonizing functions of the heart give a clear example of how to work with the universal design of the quadrants from wholeness and unity.

All information that enters your personal field is first received and recognized by your heart. Your heart always knows what is happening before your brain does. When your heart experiences harmony, it also *generates* harmony. As such, your experience of harmony can impact on the energy fields around you, and support others to also experience the *heart of Light*.

By receiving and transmitting the wave pattern that is Love, you become a catalyst for the harmony and convergence of the wave patterns that are around you and connected to you. Through your heart, you are able to directly impact on the collective field of consciousness that you are related to.

By receiving Love from, and being in resonance with, the unified field of consciousness, you can transmit Love into the collective fields of consciousness. When your inner wave patterns are coherent and harmonic, you help to actualize our Eternal qualities from within the created worlds. Restoring harmony, wholeness, and Love to our worlds begins within.

You may also understand that if you are out of harmony, and your own wave-patterns become chaotic and unbalanced, this impacts on the collective consciousness fields around you. The collective consciousness fields consist of different types of wave patterns. Some of these wave patterns have formed alliances and bonds with each other and are experienced as collective belief-systems. Many entanglements exist among the wave patterns of Light within our collective consciousness field.

The experience of collective shock, violence, and grief can quickly spread like a wave, which is registered by the heart. The heart is conscious of this even before the mind discovers what is happening. The heart's knowing ability is essential for remaining connected to and aware of each other. Be aware, however, of how your mind may respond to what is known by your heart. Conditioned responses can cause further pain and division. Your heart can observe and register the truth of what has occurred, and then respond to the pain with Love. This will aid the harmonization of the wave patterns within our collective fields that were impacted.

Remain within the Heart of Light, and find me there as YOU.

~ *Your Sun*

Letter 12
Our Freedom

My dear beloveds, now that you have heard the voices of your Mother Earth and our beautiful Sun, it is time to listen deeply to the voice of our most intimate Self - the one that is of the Eternal and beyond all concepts and forms.

In the play of consciousness, our Self takes many different shapes and forms. Its Eternal qualities can seem hidden in the cloaks of time. These cloaks of time hold different layers of a larger story of *us*. Here, in these *Letters*, we can see each other beyond these cloaks, into the heart of who we really are. Your journey and experience are unique to you. However, the journey itself belongs to all of us together.

For whatever reason you are reading this now, in whatever way Life brought you to this message, I thank you for the journey you traveled to meet me here. Between remembering and forgetting, there is a quiet, still place. In this spot resides our awareness. Feel the stillness there, pure awareness, just being. This is where we meet as One. In this space of pure awareness, you simply are. There are no expectations here, no judgments, no sorrow, just stillness, and peace. Take a deep breath into this space, my beloveds, as you relax deeply into your Self.

Irrespective of whence you have come, the color of your skin, your family name, your personal or cultural background, your history, what you have done or not done, you are welcome here. In this awareness rests the deepest knowing. This knowing does not need a name, a label, or a form. It just IS. Within this awareness, we come home. Here we rest together from our personal and collective journeys with all its tribulations and challenges. Relax, my beloveds, in this beautiful space of us.

Through our previous *Letters*, you have traveled deeply inside yourself. This has started a process, which will continue to unfold, as each new insight builds on the one preceding it. In this *Letter*, I would like to share with you more about the paradox of freedom and Love. The conditioned mind does not understand the root of freedom, since this is what it obscures.

Without the realization of Love, one cannot realize freedom either. True freedom is based on our integration, the realization of our wholeness. A person who feels the need to divide, either internally or externally, is not free. Freedom is the ability to not play into the divisional dynamics and stay close to our inner wisdom. The parts of us that may urge us to divide, deny, hide, or polarize our Eternal qualities are not the parts that are of our free Self. These parts have grown out of our conditioning, fear, and a sense of separateness.

If you employ the methods of the polarity matrix, you also reinforce it from within. Whatever we distort, whether inside or externally, becomes part of our experience and distracts from our deeper unified reality. This is the trap. In the same way, whenever we attempt to control and manipulate outcomes, we create the conditions for entrapment and ultimately suffering. We are bound by what we bind. We are controlled by what we control. Yet, is it really freedom we desire? That is perhaps the question to explore further.

The Paradox of Freedom

Freedom *from* and freedom are not the same. We all desire to experience freedom, yet most of the time this is based on the feeling that our freedom is somehow limited and constrained, due to the conditions of our world and our relationships. Paradoxically, it is this experience of limitation and bondage that gives rise to our search for freedom. The impulse for freedom is often born from experiences of unfreedom.

When we have not yet realized the root of our freedom, we follow this impulse by creating experiences that distract from our true freedom. We then become more trapped by becoming dependent on the conditions we have created for our freedom, via our conditioned mind. Ironically, in this way, we become more tied to our conditioned mind.

We cannot realize our freedom with our conditioned mind, but we can become aware of our conditioned mind. For example, our conditioned mind may reject certain experiences by providing their opposites, without addressing the pattern of rejection. Whereas, our awareness may help us become conscious of our pattern of rejection. And our wisdom may, then, urge us to embrace what we run away from. In this way, we are able to transcend and transform our own conditioning.

When we create from fear, limited perception, or division, our creations lack a foundation in Love. Love is union; it is of the Eternal. This is the root of our freedom. When we act from Love, we have the capacity to embrace even the most challenging experiences, trusting the deeper wisdom that lies underneath everything. By acting from Love, we remain connected with our Eternal nature. Love does not aim to create freedom away from something or someone. Instead, Love shows us the true nature of our bondages and limitations and their purpose. By realizing the roots of our suffering, we give rise to deep compassion.

In the conditioned world, Love and freedom are often played out in opposites. Sometimes to the point of being contrasted as a polarity, as if one cannot have both. What remains obscured in these conditioned experiences is the true nature of a *bond*. By loving, we create and deepen our bonds with others. These bonds can sometimes become bondage. For some, this may be the reason to start exploring our exercise of freedom.

Remember when I shared with you that the Light needs to be contained and received to be made Self-aware? When this containment becomes too constraining to support the growth impulse of our embodied Light, the impulse to separate, or move *out* or *away from*, arises. When the mother's womb can no longer support the growing child, it signals the time for birth and the emergence of new life from the mother's womb.

When we feel contained in a limiting and conflicting way, this is often the result of agreement structures of control and distrust, not Love. How can we respond to this without becoming further entangled in it? By trying to break away from *that*, are we not also empowering *it?* Our Self-realization grows through contrasting experiences, when it does not further feed our conditioned mind. This is the greatest challenge.

When we understand that the realization of our freedom can take place within any experience, and thus our experience can neither constrain nor cause it, something deep inside shifts. When my children were captured as slaves, many of them realized that the chains that were violently forced on them could not deny them their true freedom. Those who led the resistance movement to these unacceptable practices often found strength and courage by realizing the true nature of freedom. They knew that even when their life was brutally taken, their Spirit would remain free. This strength and deep inner knowing kept their minds free.

Freedom, my beloveds, as you can see, is not an experience. What you experience is the context, the conditions, and the contrast that give rise to the deeper questions that free our minds. Would you be able to explore your freedom without contrast, bondage, and limitation? Would you even know the concept of freedom if there were no restrictions at all? Although our nature is of the Eternal and essentially free, the paradox of freedom is that we do not become aware of this directly. We can begin to recognize the difference between projection and direct perception only when we understand our conditioning.

When we do not initially recognize our unity and pure consciousness, we condition our minds with all kinds of projections. Then, we create by our conditioning until something in us awakens and starts to realize our conditioning. This then serves as further ground for deeper awakening and Self-realization. Thus, the realization of our freedom requires awareness of conditioning first. The One that is aware of conditioning is also the One that is free. Does a computer know it is conditioned and limited by its designer? Is it Self-aware of its condition, its program? Can it choose to obey or disobey its program? Or, is that option of perceived choice also programmed into it?

Experience is formed by our minds and influenced by our perception. But what causes this perception? If our sense of Self is fabricated by our mind, and the mind itself is conditioned by its experiences, how then can freedom be realized by our mind? What in us remains free, irrespective of our conditions, and is unconstrained by what we think or believe? Reflect on this: What in you is aware of these limitations? What in you is aware of thought itself? Is it the mind? Or, is it the awareness in which the experience of mind arises? Just pause in that realization, so you can better understand causation.

Does your mind, and all that enters into it, define you? Or, is your sense of Self based on something more fundamental? The conditioned mind is always limited; it can thus not produce, cause, or limit our freedom. And yet, we let our world and our relationships become defined, to a large extent, by the information that has been generated by our conditioned minds. The exploration and realization of these deeper questions are part of the process of the realization of our innate freedom.

There is a great liberation when we realize that the mind is *not* the source of our being, that mind can dissolve into the nothingness that gave rise to it. In this realization, there is a deep peace and stillness. Remember, the experience of the seventh ray of Light and the seventh gate? In this stillness, only pure awareness remains.

You may understand now why our fundamental freedom is not something that is created by anyone. In the same way, it cannot be taken from us. This deepens, even more, our capacity to Love. We are not our conditioning, and we should not let our conditioning define us. Your capacity to Love comes from your Eternal nature. You are free to bring that forth.

The Bonds of Love

Let us explore more deeply now, the bonds of Love. When we Love each other, and we generate or affirm our bonds, there is a willingness in this process to be constrained, to some extent, by the bonds of Love. This often serves to secure our relationships. Agreements in relationships can serve as bonding mechanisms, which can define the form of the relationship. As a result, zones of exclusivity and inclusivity are formed. Sometimes this happens consciously, and sometimes unconsciously.

For example, intimate partners may agree not to share their intimacy with each other with others. Children and parents may agree that the nature of care and responsibility is unique to their parent-child relationship. My relationship of care for each of you, as your planet, has given me the name Mother Earth, since I look after you all like a mother.

This bonding process provides a sense of connectedness, from which a deeper sense of *we* and *us* can form. Yet, sometimes the *bonding process* becomes confused with *owning*. Ownership often gives rise to the desire to claim the relationship, or the other person, as *mine* - e.g. my child, my wife, my husband, my partner, and my land. This concept of *mine* always contains unhealthy exclusivity.

It is also possible to experience healthy exclusivity without this kind of ownership. For example, secure and safe boundaries in relationships are essential for our development and growth. Your cells choose between the most useful and non-useful resources for your body's healthy functioning. This too is a process of selection by inclusion and exclusion. Yet, when exclusivity and inclusivity are used without Love, without the awareness of our underlying unity, it can create harmful divisions.

Freedom, in the context of Love, is thus not about doing whatever we want. It is a much deeper awareness and concern to act in a way that serves and honors the *good of the whole*, and our relationships within that. Sometimes these actions require a sacrifice, a voluntary giving up of what we *would* have wanted, for what is *needed*. By doing so, a deeper flourishing of each individual can become possible. When Love is the underlying motivation, we do not experience the constraints on our freedom as unacceptable. Instead, we realize that our collective freedom is about our collective liberation from the polarity matrix, by our integration and through our re-unification.

Our bondage, in positive and negative manifestation, can become the foundation for realizing our freedom and thus actualizing our Love. Remember, I shared with you that as your planet I became a safe container, a recipient of the sacred flame of Love. As a living grail, the flame becomes contained through the process of embodiment. This grail does not control the flame; it does not ask it to give up part of it Self to stay loyal to the grail. This grail holds and embodies the flame. Its boundaries and structure provide experiences that give feedback for Self-actualization.

From the perspective of Love, you may see that there are natural boundaries that serve to provide safe structures for our growth and flourishing. These boundaries will also contain, limit, and constrain activities that harm the good of the whole. When the true nature of freedom as Love has not been realized, these constraints may appear as constraints on freedom. This can give rise to a sense of polarity, or tension, between Love and freedom, as if they serve opposite objectives, which in reality they don't.

Choose the Third Way

This misconception, that Love and freedom serve different objectives, has caused much pain and suffering in our world. Some of my human children believe they must choose between Love and freedom. Love, then, represents keeping the bonds and agreements that were formed, and freedom is expressed as development and new growth. This perceived choice comes from our conditioning. By choosing one over the other, we end up feeling even more divided.

Initially, by resisting this choice, we may feel paralyzed, not knowing in which direction to move. Herein is the key, don't go in either direction. Choose the *third option*, or the middle-path, which is the trinity that removes us from our polarity. You don't need to choose between Love *or* freedom, my dearest. They both serve our unity.

Polarity perception comes from our conditioning. Reach for the center. Choose integration, and arrive in Middle Earth. There, all opposites are transcended by seeing it all for what it truly is. If you have given power to this false choice, reclaim that power now. The third choice is the real choice, by not choosing *either or.* Know this with your heart, not just your mind.

If previously you have felt tension between Love and freedom, go deeper now to realize the nature of that tension. Realize *that* Love and freedom have not produced this tension. You have! Notice now on *what* and *whom* you projected this tension. How did this tension play out in your life? Let us explore this a little further.

Our first experiences of Love often come from the bonds of care we experience with another person. These bonds may have been with your parents, caregivers, or someone else. In the experience of this kind of bond, there is often a sense of safe attachment, which can make us feel loved, seen, and protected. If this bond was consistent, while also providing space for exploration and development, it probably helped to feel a sense of *trust in Love* through relationship. If, however, this bond was inconsistent and unpredictable, lacking a strong foundation, it may have caused a feeling that Love cannot be trusted, giving rise to fear that we should never grow depended on an other.

The conditions of your first experiences of Love provide a context for the exploration of these deeper questions. The exploration of our boundaries is a natural developmental process. Without freedom, we cannot explore. Without exploration, we cannot learn. Without Love, the exploration of our freedom can be damaging, leading to pain.

Our conditioned mind distorts the true nature of our bonds, our natural interconnectedness. It is from this distortion that many *unfree* choices are made, which cause more suffering and entrapment. Explore deeply how this trap of false choices applies to you. Thinking ourselves free of this does not mean we are, even more so when the thinking process comes from our conditioning.

When Love Informs our Choices

Connect with this timeless Love inside of you. Feel it and from this Love now ask yourself: *How does my bond with this person serve us to grow individually and collectively?* Explore the nature, purpose, and agreement structures within the bonds that you have formed with others. If there are restrictions in these bonds and agreements, is that based on control and distrust? Or are these restrictions conditions for a deeper growth in the relationship?

Remember, the conditioned mind is not free. It produces more conditioning by imposing conditions that are artificial. Can you free what need not be contained? Can you contain what requires safe boundaries made from Love for healthy growth and development? Honor the wholeness of which we are a part. I, as your planet, your Mother Earth, am not your entrapment into form. Our embodiment is a sacred gift of Love. Let us bring this forth now, through our care for each other.

The Illusion of Free Choice

Everything serves a purpose, yet not everything serves the whole. In the world of time, change is the only constant. The world of time also gives us the perception that we have free choice. This perceived freedom of choice comes from seeing options and alternatives coupled with a sense of *I as the maker of that choice.* This 'I' is often limited by that which it cannot yet see. The question thus arises, whether this *limited* I can make a *free* choice?

If freedom is not an experience, but a fundamental truth of our true nature, can *free choice* be an experience? Unless we know the part of us that does the *choosing*, we may be in for a surprise. Especially when our choices create unforeseen pain and further conditioning. We cannot create freedom from a place of unfreedom, to do so would bring you deeper into polarity. You can, however, use the experience of unfreedom for the realization of freedom. This will bring you home to our Eternal nature.

As I shared before, you keep yourself free by not dividing and polarizing our wholeness. The paradox of Life is that we experience the changeless in a world of change; we experience darkness by contrast of light, and so forth. We live in a world of duality, yet underlying this is unity. That is what our trinity is all about.

When bondage is formed by Love, it serves the realization of freedom. When bondage is formed by the denial of Love, it serves the suppression of freedom. Our conditioned mind cannot create freedom. Our conditioned mind does not realize Love. It searches for it, yes. It may desire it. But it does not realize itself as that Love. When it does, conditioning ceases. Awareness is always here, nothing can obscure or obstruct it, yet we do not always recognize that our ability to see is based on *that.*

Our Nature is Love

Love embraces everything and everyone unconditionally because nothing can divide it. Love is unconditional because nothing can condition it. It is not formed nor influenced by our minds. It is not of the mind, and it is not of the temporal dimensions of our worlds. Love is from the Eternal. Its perception is always universal. Love liberates because Love is free.

Love helps you see and feel the difference between what is false and what is real. Love protects us because it keeps us connected with our Eternal nature and each other. Love protects us from the conditioning effects of our minds, not by separating from it, but by seeing it from awareness. Love does not change, and yet it causes change to happen when required for our further development and evolution. In a world that is founded on Love, there is no denial or suppression of our freedom.

When Love is our foundation, we move forward and progress by honoring it in all expressions of Life. When Love is our foundation, relationships become sacred. To exit the labyrinth, see now the whole design and the purpose it served. We are not bound by the design of the labyrinth. It produced experiences of bondage, restriction, division, entrapment, and limitation in our minds. However, just as Love cannot be changed, the design of the labyrinth cannot change *You.* You are not the experience; you are the witness of that experience. You, in the deepest sense, are not changed by what you experience. In the same way, Love is not changed by our experiences.

When I started this *Letter,* I shared that it is time to listen more profoundly to the voice of our deepest, most intimate Self. This *I am* that is our most intimate Self is undividable. I cannot be seen because I am not separate from you. I am that by which you see. Love gives us strength. Trust in this and know this with your heart.

The ocean changes in appearance. Sometimes there are powerful waves. At other times there are no waves. The waves change, yet they remain part of the ocean. Love is like that. Our experiences change, but we always remain part of the ocean of Love. We are always within the One. Nothing changes our most intimate Self; only our experience changes. Be that Love. Bring it forth, for this is our nature.

Part 5
Our Integration

Letter 13
Our Story

My beloved children, thank you for journeying with me and reading this final *Letter* of the series. We have journeyed far back in time and deeply into the sacred potentials from the unified field of consciousness. This has brought us to a deeper harmony, from where we can birth the next expression of our evolutionary potentials. Everything that unfolds and forms within the fabric of Life leaves an imprint on the blanket of time. This blanket of time is wrapped around our collective consciousness in ways that remain invisible to most. It is from this blanket that we each evolve with the potentials given to us. It is from this blanket that we weave our stories.

My final message to you, in this *Letter*, is about the *heart* of all stories. Stories provide us with context for our Self-realization, within the local and the universal dimensions of our Being. Stories can help us realize who we are, what is within us, and how we can apply our potential for good and for harm. Stories can provide us powerful contexts for realizing more deeply, and more fully, the various dimensions of our Being. Yet, once the realization takes place, the context for these stories is no longer necessary. Our Eternal Self is not contextual, and yet it can be realized from within the context that our experiences provide.

Through the previous twelve *Letters*, I shared about our journey from the alchemy of our sacred union, through the era of polarity and division, toward the inner key for finding our way back into wholeness. Our story has many layers and dimensions. As your Mother, I have experienced the unfolding of all these simultaneously. I experienced the loss of my children on one side of my body, and the gain of others on the other side of my body. It revealed the temporality of each of these experiences, and the attachment to some, over the rejection of others.

This perspective of the simultaneous arising, of all these different stories and experiences within the One, can be difficult to behold. And yet, it is from this perspective that I will share my final message here. I invite you to join me beyond the *Letters* and character lines that you have grown accustomed to. Let us unpeel these various layers to reveal the original seeds of wholeness that were never lost. These seeds were merely placed through space and time as WE became our *local selves.*

As many of you have become accustomed in our collective story, there are always characters that act to unite, and those that divide. Sometimes we play the role of both. In the same way, there are characters that help us remember who we truly are, and there are those who serve to distract us. There are times we play the role of the awakener, and there are other times that the role of the trickster and deceiver overtakes us.

Sometimes it appears more convenient to deny than to honor and behold our spiritual heritage. At other times, it may appear more compelling to be the one that shakes people into remembering who we are beyond this world. There are gains and losses in each of these characters and story lines. Within the larger scheme of things, one cannot conclude that one role is more important than the other. None of them could exist of their own accord.

Some of you, my beloveds, may have hoped that in this last *Letter* I would offer a new storyline with a happy ending for all of us. We often search for this *one* story that brings an end to all our suffering. I provided you with specific keys, in these thirteen *Letters*, to find your way home again. These keys have always been directly accessible, inside your own wisdom nature. My *Letters* merely remind you of what is already within you, to provide you easier access to that which IS. By applying these keys in your daily living, you will change the way you tell your story and OUR story. This will also change the way we see ourselves in relation to all that is and has been unfolding.

You may recall the story I shared of our new future born from a different cycle of time. This story holds the resonance codes for who we are within the One. It helps us see reality without the distortions of our polarity-matrix. Day One and night One are sacred potentials in our Dreaming of a world and future that is born from Love and wholeness.

By applying these resonance codes in your own life, remembering and applying the experience of how you felt while reading day One and night One, you will help to weave the story of our healing. Stories can provide us with powerful medicine and nourishment for our souls. Yet ultimately, the story cannot set you free. It can merely point you to the realization of your freedom. We all want an end to this suffering and division. We also want to provide space and support for the new expressions of our collective consciousness, our future children. How can we best honor their learning and discovery within the context of their free will?

The way our story evolves from the context of our collective suffering depends on how we embrace and acknowledge where we have come to. The causes of our pain and violence are complex and interconnected, in the same way that our consciousness is. My body can provide enough nourishment for all my children, without constantly sacrificing my non-human children. My body provides enough plant medicine to cure all your diseases. My knowledge has always been freely available, as the intelligence of Nature. Look, and you will find it.

Our story of our beauty, kinship, relationship, and Love has become overshadowed by the pain of thousands of years of disconnection and division. This pain stems from the plundering and extraction of my resources, for the favoring of a small group that was formed a long time ago. Your story, as my human children, now tells of the awakening from the effects of this minor group. You realize now, more than ever, the impacts that corruption of power creates. Your realization is feedback for a much deeper awakening, beyond where many can see with their human eyes.

You have begun to reclaim your powers from the systems that were designed to separate. You now speak about the plundering of our body's resources and natural Life systems. You realize that my body, as your Mother planet, can support all of us in living well. You realize that the outcomes we created are unacceptable in light of all the potentials and resources given to us as Custodians for our world. You are awakening from the dream of greed and division. And you remember a different way is possible in which all of us can flourish.

As you recall and realize what is possible and could have been co-created instead, you may experience feelings of anger, disgust, and resentment. The manipulation is extensive; it runs deep and has been very invasive. As focus from the human perspective, I can share, as your planet, that this same dynamic has been operational in other spheres. We are awakening to this together in ways that go beyond what can be shared here, through mere words.

Before we continue, let us pause here, together. Connect deeply now with the wisdom for how we can live, share, and develop our wellness, flourishing, and vitality. When you land squarely in this realization, you also understand the extent of the manipulation. You see how we were sold to a dream that was never designed to empower the whole. You see the magnitude of the slavery, in its many forms and disguises. To know which dream has real potential for our collective wellbeing, watch for any underlying patterns of manipulation. The *green dream* is also sold by some of those who have hidden agendas, to take advantage of our global crisis. They will tell you that *their* solutions will set us all free. Some of these underlying dynamics are not different from the elite's power games, just more cleverly disguised.

When people feel helpless and hopeless, it is easy to manipulate their attention by distracting them from their internal resourcefulness. This is HOW the manipulation started long ago. If we are to change that part of our story together, this is what we need to change first. To be awake to *this*, and to see *how* this also operates within the domains of our own shadows.

Your greatest protection from this manipulation, internally and externally, is by staying closely tuned to your internal wisdom, and by connecting with each other from a place of Love. As I shared previously, our direct connection with the unified field of consciousness is the real foundation for our autonomy within the One. It is through this that the Universal becomes localized as you, me, and us. When you see from this awareness, deception becomes visible, as lacking thought-forms and intentions that aim to distort these wisdom qualities.

Into the Heart of Our Story

Through the previous chapters of our story, our suffering instead of our happiness provided the strongest context for our collective awakening. We stand together now, in a time that provides profound feedback from each of these earlier learning journeys. This feedback is returning from all directions now, to the center of our collective learning space. From here the convergence is happening, by listening deeply for how this in-forms us to evolve consciously, the way we have been with each other.

As the strands of time, through our collective memories, meet each other in the center of the *Wheel of Time*, we can see that each strand brings another storyline within the larger story of our time. Each strand was woven in response to the one that preceded it. What is the strand that you hold in your hand, right now? The weaving of every new story has been made possible by the context of earlier stories. When we realize this with humility, we become more careful to lay claim that this next version of our story will change everything. Perhaps, in this humility, we find the seed for our healing and deeper awakening.

We have been driving each other apart, and we have been driving each other back together, over and over again. Our attempts at unification, and our attempts to divide, have been effective only temporarily. People who were separated from each other found ways to reunite, and those who were held together beyond their will found ways to detach from each other.

My beloveds, now you may understand why, as much I would want to share with you in the final *Letter* of this series a story about our happy ending, I cannot do so. We are together living, co-creating, and updating *our story*. Each strand in the weaving matters, and is to be honored and acknowledged for the feedback, insight, and information that it provides to the whole of us. Only then, via our integration, synthesis, and convergence can we together birth the next chapter of our collective story, as a more integrated version of ourselves.

Every attempt to change our storyline from singularity will simply repeat the patterns of the past. Our storyline will change and evolve by our integration, not by imposing on it a new storyline that is more favorable than the one we have lived previously. You may recall, the duality principle provides the context for giving us contrasting experiences from where to realize the various interwoven dimensions of our being. The trinity principle is the one that brings us back to our unity. Remember this, as you review your stories within our collective story.

Deep in the heart of our story lives a beautiful message waiting to be shared and experienced. Now is the time for us to receive, embody, and share this message, by being *who we truly are*. We are *Eternal* beings, gifted with the power of Love. Let us apply this Love now, as we come together for our healing and the restoring of our sacred harmony. My beloved, wherever you are right now, whatever your experience is right now of yourself, others, and of me as your planet, just know this is the perfect place from where to take our next step together. I am here with you and always have been. I love you deeply, and always will. Thank you for receiving my message.

~ *Mother Earth.*

About the Author

Anneloes Smitsman is a writer, storyteller, visionary, legal strategist, educator, and system developer for transformational change and whole system learning & innovation. She holds a Masters degree in Law & Political Science from Leiden University (the

Netherlands), and is currently working on her PhD thesis on systemic transformation processes at Maastricht University (the Netherlands).

She is the CEO & founder of EARTHwise Centre. She was born and raised in the Netherlands and lived there until 1996. She then went to live in South Africa, Australia, and more recently Mauritius.

Anneloes played a key role in various social change movements; providing legal and transformational strategies for how to leverage and unite local efforts with international frameworks through a shared Vision. Examples are: Le Morne UNESCO Maroon Cultural Heritage in the fight against slavery and oppression; Standing Rock and Dakota Access Pipeline; Divestment from Fossil Fuels campaigns; the Bhutan Dialogue to support healing and reconciliation for the Bhutan refugee situation; and the We Stand With Africa campaign to catalyse collective support for the famine crisis.

Anneloes developed the Education for Sustainability programme when she worked as Director at ELIA-Ecological Living In Action. She continues to lead this programme today from EARTHwise Centre, which has served as a model for whole-curriculum implementation of sustainability education for the transformation of conventional educational systems.

Through her love, wisdom and insight Anneloes inspires and supports people to actualise their true potential, and work collaboratively for a world and future where all of us can flourish. For more information visit earthwisecentre.org

About the Paintings

The paintings in this book are the original works of Rachel Tribble. After learning about *Love Letters from Mother Earth*, she felt inspired to contribute these paintings in recognition and honoring of the same voice and vision that inspires her Art. The paintings are included here in black-and-white version. We have included the paintings in such a way that you may color-in these paintings to personalize this book with your favorite colors. To see the original colors of her paintings you can visit earthwise-centre.org and racheltribble.com.

About Rachel Tribble

Rachel Tribble's award-winning artwork has captured a world-wide audience from corporations to private collectors. Her dream-like paintings are regarded as *heartfelt* and *esoteric* and are recognized for their meditative quality as emotional experiments in color and light. In the late 90's, Rachel took a hiatus from her life as a professional artist to live and work within the Native American community, where she entered an inspiring journey that took her deeper into the natural world. Inspired by the world of the Anishinaabe and Lakota people, Rachel returned in 2003 to her familiar roots as a painter.

Rachel has been featured in art books and national magazines, and her work has been gifted to nominees of the Academy Awards, the Emmy Awards, and the MTV Movie Awards. In

2008 her work for the Epcot International Flower and Garden Festival poster won the IFEA Gold Pinnacle Award for the Walt Disney Company. In 2009 she was awarded the Atlanta Design Center's Visual Display Award. In 2012 and 2013 her work was in the Red Dot and Spectrum shows during Art Basel in Miami. Rachel is the co-founder of The Association for Tribal Heritage, dedicated to Native American cultural preservation and education. For more information visit racheltribble.com

77611090R00088

Made in the USA
Lexington, KY
29 December 2017